JAKE

Leon O. Jacobson, M.D.

JAKE

Leon O. Jacobson, M.D.

*The Life and Work of a
Distinguished Medical Scientist*

Eugene Goldwasser

Science History Publications/USA
Sagamore Beach
2006

First published in the United States of America
by Science History Publications/USA
a division of Watson Publishing International
Post Office Box 1240, Sagamore Beach, MA 02562-1240, USA
www.shpusa.com

© 2006 Watson Publishing International

If the publishers have unwittingly infringed the copyright in an illustration reproduced, they will gladly pay an appropriate fee on being satisfied as to the owner's title.

All rights reserved. This book may not be reproduced, in whole or in part, in any form (beyond that copying permitted by Sections 107 and 108 of the U.S. Copyright) without written permission from the publisher.

Library of Congress Cataloging-in-Publication Data

Goldwasser, Eugene.
   Jake, Leon O. Jacobson, M.D. : the life and work of a distinguished medical scientist / Eugene Goldwasser.
      p. cm.
   Includes index.
   ISBN 0-88135-279-9 (alk. paper)
   1. Jacobson, Leon O. 2. Medical scientists—United States—Biography.
I. Title.

R154.J3614G65 2006
610.92—dc22   2006042369

Design and typesetting by Publishers' Design and Production Services, Inc.
Manufactured in the U.S.A.

Contents

	Foreword	vii
	Acknowledgments	x
	Dedication	xi
Chapter One	From Poison Gas to Cancer Cure	1
Chapter Two	On the Ranch	7
Chapter Three	College Student and Teacher	15
Chapter Four	Medical School	21
Chapter Five	The Atomic Bomb Project	25
Chapter Six	A Seductive Idea that Led down the Wrong Path and away from the Nobel Prize	29
Chapter Seven	Argonne Cancer Research Hospital	37
Chapter Eight	Erythropoietin	47
Chapter Nine	Administrator, Chairman, and Dean	57
Chapter Ten	Jake the Person	65
Chapter Eleven	Last Days	77
	Index of Names	81

Foreword

Who was Leon O. Jacobson? There are no diseases to which his name is attached, no treatments named after him, and no hospitals or institutes with his name on the façade or letterhead. His contemporaries in medical science are now mostly gone, with few remaining to attest to the impact he had during his professional life. He frequently spoke, with admiration, about people he called three-headed monsters: those who were gifted at science, teaching, and patient care. In his case, a fourth head, administration, must be added.

How he is remembered depends on which of the four heads is involved. Former patients might recall him as an exceptionally empathetic doctor who was tireless in treating their illnesses and who remained a friend long after their therapy was over. Former medical students knew him as a dedicated academic clinician who taught them compassion by example along with clinical hematology and experimental science and as the faculty member who greatly encouraged student research by establishing a forum in which they could present their work in their last year in medical school. Former colleagues in the Department of Medicine at the University of Chicago knew him first as head of hematology then as chairman of a large department replete with fractious clinicians and scientists, some of whom took issue with his attempts to improve the department. Former faculty members of the Division of Biological Sciences knew him as an informal Dean who could, with grace, weather the continuous academic storms and who, unlike his predecessors, nurtured the basic biological sciences and at the same time worked to build up the clinical sciences. Former donors to the university knew him as the person to whom they could not say no. Those who worked with him at the Argonne Cancer Research

Hospital, of which he was founder and director, knew him as a friendly boss who was supportive with funds, space, and advice. They also knew him as a generous administrator who was willing to take chances on people and help them do their best research. They all learned from him how to identify and analyze problems in biology and how to design experiments. Former presidents and provosts of the university knew him as a dedicated and tireless champion of the institution, willing to extend himself when there was a chance of getting a donation. His immediate family knew him as a very busy father and husband who had little time for family life except for vacations in Michigan.

Among the many who have never heard of him, but who owe a debt to him, there are those who have been freed of the fear of dying from leukemia and related diseases, patients with successful bone marrow transplants, and people with chronic kidney disease who have a much improved everyday life in spite of their illness. They all owe a debt of gratitude to this remarkable doctor.

He made his way from a small ranch in an obscure part of the northern Great Plains to become a major figure in medical science, education, and administration, on both the national and international scene.

This book is an attempt to make Jake's life and his contributions more widely known, and to demonstrate how scientific and academic distinction is possible even for those with the most humble beginnings.

The author collaborated with Jake on research problems for many years and knew him as a scientist and administrator but not as a close personal friend. In a biography of this type, the information available, of necessity, is mostly one-sided. I relied to a significant extent on an 81-page autobiographical sketch by Leon Jacobson written in 1981 or 1982 but never circulated or published. That document is his own view of his history and does not contain any opposing views. Some of those can, however, be inferred from what documentation exists, but the record is incomplete. The collected papers in the University of Chicago archives were an important source, but once again they are one-sided. Dr. Elise Torczinski, his widow, very generously allowed me access to a large amount of personal material. His son Eric and daughter-in-law Rita also generously let me see papers in their possession and spoke very freely to me. Drs. Eric Simmons, Clifford Gurney, and Richard Landau also shared their recollections of Jake with me. I am also indebted to Alice Schreier, curator of special collections and her staff at the Regenstein Library of the University of Chicago for their help with the Jacobson archive.

Throughout his professional life Dr. Jacobson was known as Jake and I will refer to him by that name almost without exception in this account of his life.

Acknowledgments

I am greatly indebted to Dr. Elise Torczinski for permission to examine the papers kept by the University of Chicago Regenstein Library Special Collection, to Eric and Rita Jacobson for access to their papers and their willingness to participate in frank conversation, to Drs. Eric Simmons, Richard Landau, John Bonner, and Clifford Gurney for sharing their memories with me, and to Roger Becklund for information about Sims and Almont, North Dakota. The material on the Bari raid came largely from the book *Disaster at Bari* by G.B. Infield. The long quotation in Chapter One is from the paper "From Atom to Eve" by L.O. Jacobson published in *Perspectives in Biology and Medicine*. Some information came from an unpublished interview of Jake by the Columbia University oral history program. Some of the material in Chapter 7 came from a paper by Stuart Feffer in Volume 22 of the University of California (Berkeley), "Historical Studies in the Physical and Biological Sciences."

DEDICATION

To the memory of Florence Goldwasser, 1927–1980
and to my wife and constant support
Deone Jackman

CHAPTER ONE

From Poison Gas to Cancer Cure

"The patient definitely had a remission..."

In 1943, at the University of Chicago hospital, a young doctor, just a few years out of medical school, embarked on an extremely bold clinical experiment involving a very poisonous substance. This experiment led to the first use of chemotherapy in the treatment of leukemias and related diseases, ushering in a new era of cancer therapy.

During World War II, there were several government-funded, secret research labs on the University of Chicago campus. Jake was a medical advisor to one, the Toxicity Laboratory, and was deeply involved with the other one, the Metallurgical Lab. The Toxicity Lab had several sections, each involving some aspect of chemical warfare; the mission of the lab was to develop potential new chemical weapons, test them for toxicity, test compounds sent from other labs for their toxic effects, and search for agents that could possibly protect against known chemical weapons.

I first met Jake in 1943 when I was working at the Toxicity Lab prior to being drafted into the army. I had been working with a volatile arsenic compound and carelessly forgot to turn on the fume hood. When I began to feel ill, I was sent to be examined by Jake, who diagnosed a mild case of arsenic poisoning and prescribed taking a week off, going home to Kansas City, and resting. When he hired me to be on the staff of the Argonne Cancer Research Hospital some 8 or 9 years later, I found that he had no recollection of that incident, even though it still was fresh in my memory.

The research at the Toxicity Lab was in anticipation of the possible use of chemical weapons by the Germans or Japanese. In the

1914–1918 war, one of the chemical weapons used by the German army on the Western front was mustard gas, a sulfur compound that caused intense blistering of the skin, severe pulmonary damage, destruction of the blood-forming tissue, and eventually, death. During the period between wars, some analogs were synthesized using nitrogen instead of sulfur. These nitrogen mustards also caused severe blistering of the skin on contact and were also very toxic when inhaled. The mechanisms of the effects of both the sulfur and nitrogen mustards were studied intensively by the Toxicity Lab staff and investigators at other venues, in an attempt to find a way to counteract their devastating effects.

A number of sources, including Jake's own reminiscences, have suggested that an incident during the World War II Allied campaign in Italy was the initiating event that culminated in the concept of successful cancer chemotherapy. The city of Bari on the southern Adriatic coast of Italy had been captured from the German occupying force by the advancing American and British troops. Bari had a strategically important harbor that was used to land troops and materiel for the land campaign, and was frequently filled to capacity with up to 30 ships and large numbers of personnel. For the most part, the harbor was not a target for the Luftwaffe (the German air force), possibly because of what was supposed to be effective air cover by the Royal Air Force. The British commander of the RAF supporting the Allied campaign in Italy, Air Marshall Sir Arthur Cunningham, was quoted as saying at a press conference, "I would regard it as a personal affront and insult if the Luftwaffe should attempt any significant action in this area." On December 2, 1943, after German reconnaissance showed that there was no effective defense against air attack, a fleet of more than 100 German bombers raided Bari, thus affronting the Air Marshall, and causing immense damage.

There was an American Liberty Ship, the John Harvey, moored at the quayside along with many ships with oil, gasoline, and munitions as cargo. The John Harvey cargo included some materiel the nature of which was known only to a few junior army ordinance officers on board. It consisted of 2,000 aerial bombs each containing 100 pounds of mustard gas. Presumably, the mustard gas was to be used in retaliation if the retreating German army used chemical weapons against the advancing Allied troops.

Near the start of the raid, the John Harvey was hit by a bomb that caused a small fire on board. Ships all around the Harvey were being blown up or catching fire, and soon the Harvey was ablaze. The munitions in the cargo hold then blew up and the explosion killed all hands on board including the few ordinance officers who knew about the secret cargo. Among the large number of ships hit during the air raid were many carrying fuel oil and munitions. The tankers hit were set afire, while the munition carriers exploded all over the harbor. There were enormous amounts of oil on the surface of the water and the mustard gas released from the John Harvey mixed with it and was also vaporized, making the air, as well as the harbor water, toxic. Seamen escaping from the burning and exploding ships jumped into the oil-mustard mixture floating on the harbor surface, getting soaked with the poisonous stuff, all the while inhaling the toxic fumes. Due to the raid, there were about 800 casualties among the crews of the ships, including more than 600 with symptoms of mustard gas poisoning, and about 1,000 Italian civilians living in Bari were also affected. The inhabitants of Bari were first exposed to direct bombing, then to the major blasts coming from the exploding ships in the harbor. Those who went to the harbor to get water to put out fires or to wash off debris were covered with the oil-mustard mixture, all the while inhaling the toxic air. When a British officer of the port was told about the peculiar smell coming from the bombed ships, he commented that it was probably due to the garlic the Italians used so profusely.

In his writings, Jake mentioned a letter from Dr. Clarence Lushbaugh (who was part of the Toxicity Lab staff), bringing to his attention an article by C.G. Zubrod about the Bari raid. Zubrod wrote: "... noticing the devastating effects of this gas on the blood cells of men killed by the chemical, an investigating physician (Dr. S.F. Alexander) wondered whether the mustard gas might benefit patients with leukemia." Accounts of the development of cancer chemotherapy generally cite this statement as the initiation of the concept that these toxic chemicals with such a profound effect on blood cell formation could be used as a treatment for leukemia, which is characterized by overproduction of white blood cells.

While it makes a neat dramatic and ironic progression of ideas from a devastating war-time catastrophe to a treatment of a terrible disease, it just didn't happen that way. The bombing of Bari took place on December 2, 1943; however, the clinical trial described below took place eight months earlier in March of that year. The idea that overproduction of white blood cells due to leukemia might be controlled by using the toxic nitrogen mustard had to have been derived from the laboratory studies by Lushbaugh, and others, of the effects of mustard gas on laboratory animals, not from the Bari incident.

For their first clinical trial, based on the experiments on mice, Jake and Lushbaugh determined an appropriate dose regimen of the nitrogen mustard, which, because of war-time security, had to be called "compound X" but was actually the nitrogen mustard called HN2. They got permission to do the clinical test in March of 1943. In a retrospective article, Jake's description of the trial gives a vivid sense of what it was like to venture into such an uncharted area of medicine:

> It may be difficult for many to understand the deep concern one has when one is giving an extremely toxic but potentially therapeutically effective chemical to a patient for the first time. True, one has the advantage, in a deliberately planned human experiment such as this, that the dose is controlled or calculated from experience with animals and from knowledge of all the specific organ and systemic effects of a wide variety of dose schedules. Human beings generally, but not always, respond to a drug or to a toxic substance in a way similar to animals. Therefore the first trial is inevitably a time of great concern. Obviously, to proceed with this clinical trial, we had to obtain the permission of Dr. George Dick, Chief of Medicine, as well as Dr. Franklin McLean, the director of the Toxicity Laboratory. Dick was experienced as a clinical investigator, and his cautious supportive role in this venture cannot be overemphasized. The participation of Dr. Charles Spurr and Dr. Taylor Smith as part of the clinical research team was essential. Lushbaugh, with his vast biological and pathological experience with the nitrogen mustard gasses in general and with the particular one we employed, was a constant observer and advisor and, in fact, must be credited not only with the idea to proceed but with invaluable suggestions on dose schedules and possible toxic manifestations of the drug.
>
> After I gave the injection, I remained with the patient for 24 hours. Within 15 minutes the patient became extremely nauseated and for several hours had severe vomiting; but about 8 hours after the injection he was able to drink water, although he had no appetite. All

vital signs were normal and remained so. Two and 4 days after the first injection, the same dose was repeated. Each time severe nausea and vomiting followed. But the high blood count came down, and the leukemia-infiltrated lymph nodes and spleen became smaller. The patient definitely had a remission . . .

This was a patient with lymphatic leukemia, for whom all of the available therapies had failed. A second patient, this time with Hodgkin's disease, was treated with the same effects and with an even greater response: the patient went into remission, returned to his job, and lived happily for many years. Jake and his colleagues went on to treat 59 patients with HN2 and achieved the same significant success.

During the war years, there were several labs around the country working on chemical warfare problems, including the group at Yale of which Dr. Alfred Gilman was a part. They arrived at the same idea about using nitrogen mustard to treat leukemia and did a clinical trial with a different but similar compound called HN3, after having seen tumor regression in mice treated with it. They did this trial several months before Jake did his. The Yale group treated patients with lymphoma or Hodgkin's disease. Of the six terminally ill patients, none survived, but there was a striking effect on the blood-forming tissue. Because of the greater toxicity of HN3, they did not pursue those studies. Their results and those of the Chicago group were communicated to many of the investigators around the country, but because of wartime security regulations none of these results were available to the general medical profession until they were published in 1946.

The publication in the October issue of the *Journal of the American Medical Association* contained three papers, the order of which was: one by Maxwell Wintrobe et al. from the University of Utah School of Medicine in Salt Lake City, followed by that of the Gilman group, and lastly the paper from the Chicago group. Jake was bitter about the order of the papers because Wintrobe had come to Chicago to learn how to use HN2 and Jake gave him some of the compound to take back to Salt Lake City for his clinical trial. Jake thought his or Gilman's paper should have preceded Wintrobe's, but seniority seemed to have been of primary importance to the editors of the journal. The present opinion is that the Gilman group members were the originators of what eventually became cancer chemotherapy. Gilman stated, however, in a 1963 paper that "Jacobson and his associates at the

University of Chicago independently initiated therapeutic trials in 1943 . . ." These clinical experiments by both groups were the forerunners of the chemotherapy that is widely used today for treatment of some cancers and has proved to be life-saving for many patients. The credit for this innovative approach to cancer therapy must be shared between the Chicago and Yale investigators.

CHAPTER TWO

ON THE RANCH

"My life was full of the enjoyment that comes with the wide open spaces . . ."

Sims, North Dakota doesn't exist anymore except as a ghost town; it had been in the south-western part of the state near the confluence of Sims and Crooked creeks and close to Hailstone creek, about five miles north of Almont and 43 miles from Bismarck. Sims, founded in 1873, went into a steep decline when the Northern Pacific Railroad abandoned it as a fueling and watering stop. The original population was about 1,000; by 1906 there were only 300 residents and by 1970 there were four, three of whom lived in a farmhouse that was within the original town limits and a fourth who was the caretaker of the Sims Scandinavian Evangelical Lutheran Church, founded in 1884. The town officially died in 1947.

Sims is perhaps best known as the birthplace of Dr. Leon Orris Jacobson. He was born there on December 16, 1911.

The reason for Sims' existence seems to have been a lignite mine nearby. The town was founded by John Swarm and Dennis Hannafin in 1873, after they found a coal (lignite) mine in a cave. They called it Fort Hannafin and guarded their cave against Indian attack using weapons supplied to them by Col. George A. Custer's troops, who were all slain three years later at Little Bighorn. The mine, called Baby Mine, was actually opened by Col. E.H. Bly in 1881 with the intention of selling lignite mixed with bituminous coal to the Northern Pacific Railroad as fuel for locomotives. The locomotive engineers found it unsatisfactory because it was so light it flew up the stack with the smoke and could not generate enough power to get heavy loads up steep grades.

The lignite was then sold for use as domestic fuel and for stationary engines. By 1883, Baby Mine proved too expensive for Col. Bly to operate and was sold to C.J. Thompson, who had been a veins manager of the mine. He found new lignite veins near enough to the surface to reduce the cost of mining and by 1888 was selling the fuel for $1.50 per ton, by the car load lot. Since it cost $1.00 per ton to extract 25 tons a day, it was quite a profitable venture.

In addition to lignite there was a bed of good-quality clay near the mine, which provided the material for a brickyard. Sims was a rarity in that part of the Great Plains, having had many houses made of brick rather than of wood. At that time and place, brick was cheaper than wood. They shipped brick as far as Bismarck to build the North Dakota State Capitol. Another distinction for Sims was its three-story brick hotel, the largest west of the Missouri River. The hotel was famous for having an out-house on the third floor with a chute leading to ground level.

The town, by one account, was named for William S. Sims, captain of the steamship *Dacotah*; by another, it was named for George V. Sims, chief clerk of the Northern Pacific R.R. In 1911, when Jake was born there, Sims was largely agricultural, with cattle and sheep ranches as well as small farms.

Jake's family were immigrant Norwegians. His mother's parents emigrated from the south coast of Norway. His maternal grandfather, Arion Johnson, was a seaman who left his ship in San Francisco in 1850 to join the crowds in the gold rush. He stayed in California for ten years and returned to Norway with a substantial sum of money, the source of which he never disclosed. Some of the money was used to finance the family move to America in 1879 when they settled near Sims.

Jake's paternal grandparents also emigrated from the south coast of Norway in 1879 and also settled near Sims. Both families were homesteaders, and when they needed to the men worked in the lignite mine. Jake's father John married Rachel Johnson in 1897, after he had worked for a while as first mate aboard a trading vessel and had homesteaded in Iowa. He returned to North Dakota to homestead in the Sims area, had a small construction company there, and helped build the church in Sims that still stands in the empty town. He later became a Justice of the Peace.

Rachel and John had seven children—a girl Thalia, the eldest, and six boys: Arnold, Clarence, Melvin, Raymond, Leon, and Maurice. Schooling was difficult because of the need to work the ranch, but they all managed to go to school and the four younger brothers, Robert, Leon, Melvin and Ray, all finished high school. The family was religious and, as would be expected, very hard-working. Most of their socializing revolved about the church, having Scandinavian dinners and making their own music. John was reported to have had an excellent baritone voice and sang sea chanteys, Norwegian folk songs, and ballads from all around the world. Jake learned these songs and for the rest of his life, without needing any encouragement, gladly sang them at family gatherings and parties, accompanying himself on the piano. He and his brother Ray sang duets at home and on the Farmers Union Program that was broadcast on the Bismarck radio station KFYR. Sometimes all six Jacobson boys sang together, with Jake taking the bass part.

Late in his life, Jake wrote, in an account of his childhood:

> As a child and a teenager living on a small ranch by modern standards, my life was full of the enjoyment that comes with the wide open spaces and love in close knit family and friends The church was the center of life of the community—not the recreation center in most cases, but the ethical center of our lives. I think we come back again, again and again not only to visit friends and relatives, but to be reaffirmed in the values we grew up with. To sit on the top of a hill on the old home ranch and gaze out at the country-side is always an inspiration to me—decades of experience flash through one's mind and one lives again in that environment that will never be repeated— growing-up—the formative years—the period of focussing on one's philosophy, style ambitions and objectives. The opportunity to attend a country school is a unique experience that is more or less of the past as is the chance to be a teacher.

His childhood was spent doing the common farm chores—milking, chopping wood, feeding the chickens, and gathering eggs—as well as learning to drive a model T Ford. The six boys in the Jacobson family fished in the nearby creeks using bent pins as hooks and corks from medicine bottles as floats. Bait was bread dough, crickets, or grasshoppers. They hunted jackrabbits with a single-shot 22 caliber rifle, raced horses, plowed the open prairie, rode homemade sleds in winter, and used homemade skis on the hills. They played with homemade bows and arrows, learned how to use a lariat while on horseback, herded cattle, and picked flowers for teachers or mother.

Jake started school at age five in a two-room schoolhouse about a mile from the family ranch. He did well in school, skipping from grade three to grade five. He remembered his sixth-grade teacher, Andrew Willman, with great fondness. Willman had an important influence on the young Leon, especially with regard to mathematics. He convinced the young boy at age 11 to take the state exams required for graduation from elementary school and Jake passed them all while in seventh grade. He wanted to go on to high school after grade seven but his parents thought he was too young, especially since the high school was in Almont, about five miles from Sims. Jake then stayed for the eighth grade and Mr. Willman gave him special instruction in algebra, geometry, and trigonometry, as well as special reading assignments to keep him from being bored with the standard curriculum and to prepare him for high school.

At age 12, Jake was confirmed in the Scandinavian Evangelical Lutheran Church, where both English and Norwegian were used in the same service. He has said that it was the first time he had a store-bought suit. After graduation at that age, Jake went to the Almont High School, either walking the five miles, riding a bicycle or a horse, or driving a cart. When winter came, he lived in Almont, where he shared a small apartment over the bank with another student. The rent was five dollars a month. When Spring came, he went back to live at the ranch in Sims and commuted to school.

Almont High School had a number of teachers who were influential in Jake's academic development. He especially valued his English, German and math teachers. In his memoir, he wrote: "My high school years were blessed by a superb English teacher who somehow taught me how to write themes and use the King's English, an enthusiastic German teacher and a math teacher who encouraged me to go far beyond what I had already learned from a 7th and 8th grade teacher in a country school." Charles Denoyer, the principal of the school, was also the math teacher and, as was the case in elementary school, he quickly recognized Jake's ability and assigned him advanced subjects.

In his freshman year, while he was taking the state final exams for advancement to the sophomore year, he developed severe abdominal

John Jacobson as a young man, circa late 1880's.

Rachael (Johnson) Jacobson and John Jacobson sometime after 1897.

Jake at four...

Jacobson family ranch house in Sims, North Dakota, circa 1920's.

Almont High School which Jake attended from 1923–1927.

Sims School where Jake taught from 1931–1934.

pains. The principal sent him home to Sims and his parents took him to their family doctor in New Salem, who diagnosed his illness as appendicitis. He advised Jake's mother to take him to Bismarck for surgery. They took the only train, a very slow milk train, to Bismarck, but on the way the pain eased considerably. At the clinic in Bismarck, it was determined that the appendix had ruptured and he was taken immediately to surgery for the appendectomy. In the operating room, the surgeon and nurses prepared him for the operation then recited the Lord's Prayer in the operating room. Even in this pre-antibiotic era, he recovered completely. Back in Almont, he was able to take those exams he had missed in July and passed without any difficulty.

Jake also took courses in animal husbandry, nutrition, and stock judging. In his last year in high school, he was chosen to represent Almont High School in the state stock-judging contest in Fargo. His performance was good, except in sheep judging. As Jake later told the story:

> I will never forget this particular contest because, after judging the sheep in the ring as best I could, I finally arrived before the contest judges and presented my findings from my notes. I was asked several questions. The judges seemed to be really enjoying my presentation and the answers I gave to their questions. They were smiling and nodding their heads. That made me think I must really be doing a great job or something. Then it was over, and the leader of the judging committee asked me "Did you have much experience and practice in judging sheep?" I frankly told them that my only experience had been one two-hour session with the supervision of my school principal (whose training had been in the humanities plus some reading on the subject of sheep). Then he said, "You really did a good job of judging, but you described the calving of the wethers (castrated males) in your flock which were in fact males." I was somewhat embarrassed, having grown up on a ranch with animals; but sheep are somewhat different from hogs or horses or cattle: The wool covers a lot of things.

The high school offered an elective course in boxing given by the principal. Jake took the course, claiming that he was a pretty good boxer because of frequent sparring with his brothers. While boxing with the principal, he hit him hard enough to knock him down and on the way down Mr. Denoyer hit his head on a radiator. Jake and the radiator had knocked the principal out cold. None of the students in the room knew what to do other than to chill a towel with snow and apply it to his head. He finally did get up and except for a headache had no ill effects. He never held it against Jake. Had Jake known then what he learned later in medical school he would have been very worried about the possibility of serious injury to the head.

While in high school, Jake became aware of girls and found one greatly to his liking. His interaction with her took place under the watchful eyes of her parents. When, on occasion, he was invited to dinner at their home, he would stay for a while in the evening, either studying with her, listening to music, or sometimes "holding hands." At about nine, her mother would signal the end of the evening activities by whistling. They went to different colleges and the romance became only a memory.

He has described being taken, during this time, to country dances by his parents. The women sat on one side of the hall, the men on the other, but nobody was left out of the dancing. Music was supplied by piano, violin, drums, and saxophone all playing the melody in the same key without any attempt at orchestration.

One of the bankers on the floor below the apartment in Almont developed an interest in the twelve-year-old student and he and Jake played a game for several years. The banker would set a mathematics problem for the boy to solve and Jake would then set a problem for the banker to solve. When the time came to think about the possibility of going to college, this man arranged for the bank to lend Jake $180. This was in 1928, just before the economic crash, and by the time the loan was to be fully repaid the bank had closed, but Jake was still responsible for repaying the loan.

CHAPTER THREE

College Student and Teacher

"An unsuccessful North Dakota chicken farmer"

Success in high school and the encouragement of his teachers and parents led to his applying to North Dakota Agricultural College (now North Dakota State University) in Fargo, with the intention of getting a degree in agriculture. During the dust bowl era and even before the onset of the depression, the Jacobson family was not able to fully support him in college, but they did find resources enough to let him matriculate in September of 1928. Rachel, on occasion, would send him money from her sale of cream, and the siblings contributed what they could. One brother planted seven acres in flax with the intention of sending Jake the proceeds of his sale. The dust bowl conditions made the crop a failure but a check for $49 was sent anyway. Jake believed that the money must have come from some other source since the yield of flax was so poor.

He has related one incident that illustrates the flavor of that period. At the time of the Christmas vacation in 1929, he met an elderly lady at church, a Mrs. Charley Jacobson (no relation). She was very proud that a local farm boy was going to college and told him that she knew how expensive it was and would help him out. She gave him a dollar. Jake realized that a dollar was a lot of money in those days to both of them.

In Fargo, he lived in a private home not far from the campus with a roommate he described as a juvenile alcoholic who did not last long at the college. Fargo was a metropolis; it had a population a thousand times larger than that of Sims, and big-city amenities such as a movie house and street cars. He did so well in the English placement exam that he was enrolled in an advanced course, mainly as a result of the excellent preparation he had received from the Almont High School English teacher. The first year saw him excelling in mathematics, German, and agricultural courses. He never mentioned it in his writings, but Reserve Officers Training Corps was mandatory at the college so he also received some military training while at Fargo.

On the first Christmas break, on the way home he stopped in Bismarck to interview for a summer job in the North Dakota State Regulatory Department. In the face of stiff competition, he got the job as assistant chemist working under Dr. Culver Ladd, an organic chemist who was "very strict and exacting; a disciplinarian." He kept the job for five summers. Although he has not described what sort of testing work he did—the agency tested fuels, food, and paints for compliance with state standards—this experience of having to be "strict and exacting" must have played a role in his later life as a scientist and in the way he ran his own research laboratory.

The first two years at college were gratifying, but the economic crash and following Depression made it impossible for the family to continue to support him, and the part-time work did not allow him to earn enough to meet his needs. He had to leave college and look for a paying job. Finding work was far from easy but he was fortunate in the help he got from the college faculty, and managed to get an interview with the North Dakota Superintendent of Public Instruction. Even without having taken the usual course work required for teachers, he got a position teaching in an elementary school not far from Sims.

For the next three years, Jake taught in a two-room schoolhouse with a barn and with a creek running through the 20-acre schoolyard. He was the only teacher for 28 students in all eight grades at a salary of $80 per month. One room was used for classes and the other for non-scholastic activities such as sewing, which was taught by the students' mothers, and shop training. It was also used as a study room for the 7th and 8th graders to insulate them from the lower grades. The school had no indoor plumbing. It did have two pipe organs, one in each room, that Jake played to accompany the children when they sang songs.

It must have been grueling to juggle the eight grades, keep the children content, and still teach them something. Jake said the years teaching in that school were, in many ways, the most rewarding three years of his life. In an interview many years later, in 1966, he said that one of his successes as a teacher was with the son of the owner of the local saloon and brothel. He said the boy might have given up on an education had Jake not gotten him interested in wildflowers. While this may have been indicative of the time and place, it had to be an invention, since he also has said that Sims in the late 1920s consisted of only an abandoned railroad depot and a general store. The population was probably less than that of Almont (100) and could hardly have supported a saloon and brothel.

The teaching experience most likely sparked his later interest in medicine, since he had to deal with children with a variety of health problems, such as the common cold, bronchitis, whooping cough, measles, chicken pox, mumps, and fractures, and one child with epilepsy.

He usually started the day by reading to the students as well as supervising their outdoor play. The job also entailed keeping the furnace stoked and the school warm, and carrying water for the wash stand. He could sometimes convince a parent to bring water in a milk can.

In his third and last year of teaching in this school, and with the approval of the superintendent of schools, Jake organized a school-wide project of raising chickens for profit. The school bought a brooder and chicks, and the students learned to take care of the flock, to keep the place clean, and how to make money by raising and selling chickens. At the end of the school year, with the students all dispersed, there was a problem of what to do with the leftover chickens. Jake could not stay in Sims since he had to go to Bismarck for his summer job, so he decided to sell the chickens; but too late. Minks had gotten into the barn and killed all the birds. All that was left was to bury the carcasses and take the loss. He later described himself "as an unsuccessful North Dakota chicken farmer."

During his second year of teaching at the elementary school, on the Christmas holiday, he went rabbit hunting on horse-back. It was very cold and snowy and the horse slipped on a slope, falling with Jake on it. His left leg was broken and the horse was standing near but too far for Jake to get to it and remount. He sent the horse home and in great pain crawled about a quarter of a mile to the nearest road. The cold was so intense he worried about falling asleep and freezing to death, but the pain was also intense and kept him conscious. Eventually some people in a car found him in the middle of the road and brought him back to the ranch, where his horse was waiting. His brothers, upon seeing the horse without him, were about to set off in search when the driver of the car delivered him. The local doctor put his leg in a cast and when the holiday was over he went back to teaching. This incident, coming as it did at the time when he was debating whether to go to medical school instead of continuing in agriculture, may also have played a key role in his decision for a career in medicine.

Jake had deposited his savings from the teaching job in the bank in Almont while he was paying off the loan. When the bank closed, he still was responsible for the loan but lost all of his savings. Between the summer job and teaching he did accumulate enough money to return to college, albeit still needing a part-time job.

Over the three years of teaching elementary school, Jake's idea about his future life underwent a discreet change and he decided to apply to medical school after getting his Bachelor of Science degree. The courses he had already taken were not the ones he needed for that degree, and he set about making good his deficiencies. One course in particular was a problem; due to a scheduling difficulty, he had to take a physics course with the engineering students rather than the less demanding one with the agriculture students. It was a trying time, but with the unexpected help of the physics professor he weathered the storm. He had not passed the course but the professor offered to overlook the poor performance and give him a grade of 70, which was just passing, if he promised to be a medical missionary. Jake made the promise and later reconciled this promise with the fact that he "never went to Africa," which is what the professor intended, but ". . . kept my promise in the sense that I have preached medicine and medical science every day of my life since that interview."

On returning to Fargo for his third year at North Dakota Agricultural College, Jake got a job working for the chairman of the History department, abstracting book reviews from the *New York Times* and other periodicals. He also joined a fraternity, Theta Chi, and met his future wife Elizabeth Benton (Betty), who was the sister of a fraternity brother and a second-year student. Betty's father, Alva Benton, an agricultural economist who directed the college agricultural research station, was in Washington working for the Roosevelt administration Department of Agriculture while his wife and Betty stayed in Fargo. When it seemed clear that Betty and Jake were seriously interested in each other, her mother, apparently concerned about the seven-year age difference between them (Betty was 17), asked to talk with Jake privately. "She asked me such questions as did I drink, did I gamble, did I believe in God, and did I go to church, all of which I answered in the affirmative." The next year Mrs. Benton went to Washington, leaving Betty to room with Dr. Hunter, who was Jake's boss in the History department. At the end of that academic year, Betty joined her parents, and in the autumn of 1935 Jake went to Chicago to enter the University of Chicago School of Medicine. The separation was not particularly stressful because they kept in close touch with each other.

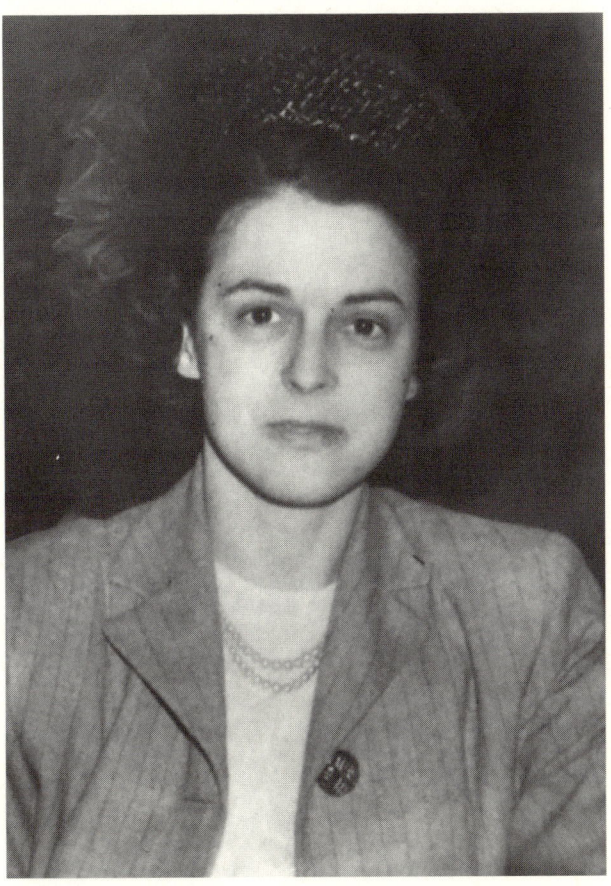

Betty Benson Jacobson at the age of thirty, a decade after she married.

CHAPTER FOUR

Medical School

"The bank in Minneapolis surely couldn't have closed . . ."

Jake has said that he applied to only one medical school, and that was at the University of Chicago. Some questions naturally come to mind: In 1935 was admission to a high-quality medical school so non-competitive that he could be sure of admission to the only one he chose despite coming from a small agricultural college? Why did he choose the University of Chicago? Did the faculty of North Dakota Agricultural College convince him that the University of Chicago was the place for him? Were there other influences related to his choice? He has written that "many of my professors were alumni of the University of Chicago," but except for that statement his writings and speeches are silent on this subject. His application form for the University of Chicago medical school has no clue about his choice; it does not contain any of the required reference letters, which are routinely discarded after a number of years, although he later acknowledged the fact that the college faculty and Dr. Culver Ladd (the person who directed his summer laboratory job in Bismarck) were helpful.

Some years later he wrote about the time he finished his Bachelor's degree: "My problem, above all else in my junior and senior years of undergraduate college, was to gain entrance to a medical school and mobilize the where-with-all to finance four more years of education." These financial matters seemed to be settled fairly easily but, in view of his concern about money, it is surprising that on his application to Chicago, in answer to the question "Will you be able, if admitted, to meet expenses, without any outside work for self-support?" he answered "yes."

He applied for and received a scholarship from the Leopold Schepp Foundation. He was also advised, possibly by his future father-in-law, Alva Benton, to write to a Mr. Shreve Archer in Minneapolis for a loan. Mr. Archer asked for Jake's college record and a brief account of himself, both of which were sent to him quickly. After some further correspondence, Archer asked him for a one-paragraph note stating his needs for the four years of medical school. The Dean of Students at Chicago suggested that Jake would need $650 per year, and Jake communicated that number to Mr. Archer. The first check came soon after, with the notice that the loan would bear 5% interest and would be payable starting at the time of graduation. He also received a one-half tuition scholarship from the University.

Jake came to Chicago in September 1935 and checked into the Stevens (now the Conrad Hilton) Hotel, at that time the largest hotel in the world. Following Mr. Archer's advice, he presented the check for $650 to the Continental Bank for deposit the next morning.

> I presented myself at a teller's window and said that I wished to open an account. The teller looked at the check, and finally said: "In order to open an account here, you have to make an application with references." It wasn't quite the same as at the bank in Almont, North Dakota. He asked if I knew Mr. Archer, and I said I had never met him, but had been in touch with him for some time, and that he had suggested I open an account with the Continental. The teller said, "Just wait here a moment and I'll be right back." He returned in a few minutes and said, "One of our senior officers wishes to see you." I immediately thought terrible thoughts, such as, the bank in Minneapolis surely couldn't have closed, etc. I was ushered into a very impressive office, a vice-president welcomed me, and our conversation began. Did I know Mr. Archer? Had I ever seen him in person? Finally, I told him the whole story. To this day, I don't know whether they worried that I had come with a forged check, or that a visit with a senior officer was a courtesy because, as it turned out Mr. Shreve Archer was a member of the Board of Directors of the Continental Bank of Chicago. The vice-president told me they would be glad to have me bank with them in spite of the fact that I couldn't possibly meet the balance requirements. He told me that he had gotten his degree in Business Administration from the University of Chicago, and that the University Bursar's office would take care of my banking needs without a balance requirement.

Mr. Archer was the Archer of the agribusiness giant Archer, Daniels, Midland Corporation. Four years later, after receiving the M.D. degree, Jake wrote to Archer to tell him about his plan to stay in Chicago for his internship, and got a reply offering congratulations and cancellation of the debt. Although the two never met, Jake felt gratitude to such an extent that many years later he established a loan fund for medical students in the name of Shreve Archer.

Arriving on campus, Jake was housed in Hitchcock Hall, a dormitory very convenient to the medical school. His roommate this time was also a student from North Dakota. Because of his deficiency in biology courses, he had to take a course in physiology in addition to the first year medical courses. That course reinforced his enthusiasm for his new adventure and sparked an interest in research in biology. In the same year, he took a course with Prof. William Bloom that started his long-term interest in blood cell formation.

In this first year of medical school, Jake was exposed to laboratory research in the lab of Dr. Jules Masserman, a psychiatrist. His work as a paid assistant involved study of the effects of alcohol and other drugs on the function of cat brains. He stayed with the problem for some time and was a co-author of the resulting paper in 1940. He has never mentioned it, but this experience must have had a profound effect on him because he stayed with laboratory research throughout his career. Another student research experience with Dr. Clarence Hodges, chairman of the Department of Radiology, in which he took X-rays of lab animals, was the basis for a major change in his life and led to his appointment to the staff of the Metallurgical Lab a few years later.

At that time, the University of Chicago had two medical schools, one on the main campus in Hyde Park on the south side of the city, and the other (Rush Medical College) on the near west side near the county hospital. The students could elect to transfer to Rush after two years, but Jake opted to stay in Hyde Park. At this time, he received a full-tuition scholarship. The class was small (38) and he took courses and interacted with some of the more eminent medical scientists in the country. Among them were Charles Huggins, Lester Dragstedt, George Dick, Franklin McLean, Walter Palmer, Joseph Kirsner, Clarence Hodges, and Stephen Rothman, all of whom remained long-time friends. They were all involved with clinical care, teaching, and research and became role models for the rest of Jake's professional life. He would describe them as "three-headed monsters."

During his third year, Betty and Jake decided to get married, but he needed the permission of the medical school Dean of Students. The Dean at the time, Dr. Basil Harvey, had no objection and so they were married in March of 1938.

Jake's persistent fascination with tissue structures, function, and pathology, especially of the blood-forming system, was whetted by course work with Drs. Bloom, Wells, Cannon, Steiner, and Humphreys. The years of clinical study exposed him to a wide variety of patients and diseases of the blood, as well as to research on that system. He started on a path from which he did not deviate during the rest of his life and which dominated his professional career.

Having decided to stay in Chicago for his internship, he was accepted to work under the direction of Dr. George B. Dick, then chairman of the Department of Medicine. It was a busy and exacting year characterized by freedom to learn and to deal with patients in an independent manner.

Dick was an authority on infectious diseases and Jake did a large number of bacterial cultures from various parts of the patients' anatomy. In a routine meeting with Dick, Jake suggested that they do a study of the data from all of those cultures; Dick agreed and they published the result in 1941 in a paper on "Normal and abnormal bacterial flora of the nose." It was during this period that he took care of a patient with Albers-Schonberg (marble bone) disease; the sequel to this study also had an impact on his later research on blood cell formation by the spleen and bone marrow.

When his internship was completed in 1940, he stayed on as a resident in Medicine. During this time, with the American entry into World War II, Jake's life changed significantly. He became involved in another of the top-secret war-time projects on campus.

CHAPTER FIVE

The Atomic Bomb Project

"I blanched, had a lump in my throat..."

IN 1942, WHEN HE WAS A SECOND-YEAR resident in Medicine, Jake was engaged in treating a patient when he heard his name on the hospital page system instructing him to go to Dean William H. Taliaferro's office. Jake knew who the Dean was but had never met him and was concerned that he might have done something very wrong and was in trouble, otherwise why would the Dean want to see someone as insignificant as a very junior member of the hospital staff. In the Dean's office were three people he knew: Dr. Dick, chairman of Medicine; Dr. Arthur C. Bachmeyer, Director of the hospital; and Dr. Hodges, with whom Jake had worked as a technician doing x-ray studies of laboratory animals while he was in medical school. There were also two people he had never seen before. The Dean greeted him with "Hello Leon" and introduced him to the two people he did not know, Mr. Norman Hilberry and Mr. Ernest Wollan, both physicists. Jake's first thought was that only his wife and mother-in-law ever called him Leon; to all others he was known as Jake, Dr. Jacobson, or as one child called him, Dr. Drake.

The two physicists were identified as being part of a project headed by Arthur H. Compton, a very distinguished cosmic ray physicist and Dean of the Division of Physical Sciences at the University of Chicago. Jake was told that Compton needed his help in the project and that Hilberry and Wollan would explain all about it to him. Jake wondered what in the world he, a young second-year resident in medicine, might be able to do to help these high-powered types in some physics project. The Dean explained that Compton's group was working with radiation from a cyclotron and with radioactive substances, and since Jake had some experience with radioactive phosphorous used in some treatments of various diseases affecting blood cell formation and with X-radiation, based on his work with Dr. Hodges he was the person they needed. In addition, he had experience with the blood-forming system based on some research he had done but not yet published, and that too would be useful. All of this related to the possibility that people on the project might have been exposed to radiation and that it was important to know about it before they were exposed to additional radiation. Jake was being co-opted for the job and agreed to do it without any idea of what it was all about and how much effort would be needed.

He was told that the work was essential to the war effort. It was, at that time, an open secret that there was, on the campus, a very extensive research program in physics called the Metallurgical Laboratory, the nature of which was known only to those actually working there. It was in fact the Chicago part of the Manhattan Project that led to the first chain-reacting atomic reactor and eventually to the atomic bomb. Jake understood he was to take care of clinical monitoring of the Met Lab personnel even though he had no clear idea of what they might be doing.

He would be given some lab space and would have a clinic available to him for examining the Met Lab workers. After the meeting with the Dean, Jake, Wollan and Hilberry went off to talk further about what he would be expected to do. Jake's "office" was a small room shared with several cages of experimental mice and the odor of mice permeated the place. For those not used to mouse smell (and even for those who were), it was too unpleasantly pervasive. This second meeting did not last long. During some meetings later at a mouse-free office, Jake became aware that his questions about the project were all answered in an evasive manner. After meetings in which Jake asked specific questions without getting clear answers, he persisted and Hilberry administered the oath of secrecy and gave Jake a physics text to read. He found that the work of the Metallurgical Lab concerned nuclear fission and the chain-reacting atomic pile. It was a dramatic moment when Jake realized that he was part of the team, headed by Enrico Fermi, that was building the first atomic reactor and was directly involved in the production of plutonium and an atomic bomb. As Jake remembered it, the book handed him by Wollan stated in essence: "If some morning you should awaken and find half of the world blown away, you will know that a nuclear fission chain reaction has been accomplished." He also remembered that he blanched, had a lump in his throat, was speechless for a time and at the point of tears. It had hit him "... with my hands down." He felt involved to such an extent that he could not get out of it. The Metallurgical Lab was a euphemism for the Chicago part of the nation-wide Manhattan Project. The chain-reacting pile produced massive amounts of radioactive materials, and the separation of plutonium from the reactor was accompanied by very large radiation doses. Security was so stringent he could not tell Betty about his new job and he had to be evasive in answering her questions. After the bomb was dropped on Hiroshima in 1945, he could break three years of secrecy and tell her what the Met Lab was all about.

Because the reactor produced such massive amounts of radioactivity and the chemical work on plutonium also involved possible exposure to a lot of radiation, he realized how important it was to keep a check on the health of the Metallurgical Lab people, and he personally did many of the physical examinations, including, as he said, those of "... Fermi, Teller, Franck, Hogness, Zachariesen, Szilard, Zinn and Seaborg." As the project grew in size and because everyone who had any possible exposure to radiation had to be examined and have blood tests done on a routine basis, the task became enormous. When he started, the only way to assess exposure to potentially dangerous radiation was to monitor the white blood cell count and look at the skin of the person. The former would be depressed significantly and the latter would be reddened. The burden was eased a bit when the physicists developed non-clinical methods, using devices worn by the staff, to detect individual exposure to radiation. The medical staff grew along with the rest of the project and Dr. Robert Stone was appointed Director of Health and Biology, with Dr. Kenneth C. Cole Co-director in charge of non-medical aspects. Jake, who was the first to be appointed, was Health Officer. The staff of doctors, investigators, and technicians grew rapidly until by the end of that year it exceeded 400. Among these who worked directly with Jake were Dr. Eric Simmons, Mrs. Edna K. Marks, and Ms. Evelyn Gaston, all of whom remained part of Jake's research group until his and their retirements.

Included in the many difficulties was that of scheduling examinations. Jake was determined not to keep people like Fermi and Szilard waiting in the clinic when they had work of such importance to do and made sure that they were scheduled without any waiting time. The nation-wide Manhattan project was expanding at a great rate and new laboratories were brought into being at sites around the country. In addition to their clinical duties, Jake and Edna Marks trained the technicians who would monitor the radiation exposure of the personnel at places like Oak Ridge, which was separating U-235, and Hanford, which was producing plutonium for bomb making.

With his growing staff doing much of the routine work, Jake had time for scientific problems associated with radiation injury. The Metallurgical Lab staff and investigators all over the country working on the Manhattan Project compiled a massive amount of data on the biological effects of radiation and of the isotopes generated in the reactor. This compendium is now available in science libraries. As the Chicago branch of the project expanded, Jake became part of the research team working at Site B, a former brewery and stable not far from the university campus. It was at Site B that Jake started his long-term collaboration with Eric Simmons, who was brought to Chicago from the University of Indiana by Ray Zirkle, who was one of the senior investigators studying the biological effects of radiation.

While at Site B, Jake started his research on the effects of radiation on blood cell formation, and organized the team of co-workers who stayed part of his research efforts for more than 30 years. He was careful to always include their names in reports and publications resulting from their work and maintained a close personal relationship with them. He also kept in contact with the large number of investigators, both junior and senior, who were part of the Manhattan Project and whose work intersected with his. These became lasting friendships.

CHAPTER SIX

A Seductive Idea that Led down the Wrong Path and away from the Nobel Prize

". . . this was the first time that anyone had saved the life of a lethally irradiated animal."

In December of 1990, in Stockholm, the Nobel Prize in Medicine or Physiology was awarded to Dr. E. Donnall Thomas of the Fred Hutchinson Cancer Center in Seattle and Dr. Joseph E. Murray of Harvard University Medical School in Boston. The citation read: "For their discoveries concerning organ and cell transplantation in the treatment of human diseases." Don Thomas was honored for his critical studies on bone marrow transplantation. Years of experimental studies by several investigators laid the foundation for Don Thomas' very important work. Among the studies were Jake's investigations of the effects of radiation on the blood-forming system, research he had started at Site B.

While his early academic interests were somewhat varied, Jake soon settled on hematology as the primary focus of his research as well as his clinical practice. His interest in the field was a result of his experience while a house officer with a patient with Albers-Schonberg's [marble bone] disease, a rare genetic disease characterized by bone overgrowth that wipes out that portion of the bone marrow where blood cells are formed. This disease is often accompanied by development of lymphoma. Evidence in the literature showed that mice given large doses of estrogen showed increased bone growth, as in the human disease, but did not develop lymphomas. Jake, after seeing that patient, decided to reinvestigate the inter-relationship between bone formation and the production of blood cells.

Among Jake's earliest publications was an experimental study of the effect of repeated large doses of estradiol (estrogen) administered to mice in an attempt to understand why females have fewer red blood cells than males. As was already known, the estrogen had the property of causing increased formation and deposition of bone mineral, especially in the hollow space occupied by the blood-forming cells of the marrow. In the estrogen-treated mice, this crowding of the marrow space by new bone caused decreased red blood cell formation by that tissue and yet the animal did not become anemic. There was, instead, a compensatory increase in blood cell formation by the spleen resulting in essentially a normal red blood cell count. These experiments were the point of departure for a series of extended studies of the relative roles of the spleen and bone marrow in blood cell formation and led to his work on the possibility of reversing the lethal effects of radiation injury.

The Metallurgical Lab team had found a much more severe effect of radiation on the blood-forming system of laboratory animals than on almost any other organ system of the body. The primary early cause of death due to x-rays and other radiation was the destruction of the capacity to make blood cells. Continuing his experiments on blood cell formation, Jake studied the results of administering the radioisotope, 89-strontium to mice.

Strontium is chemically very similar to calcium, a normal constituent of bone mineral, and, when in the blood stream, is treated like calcium, i.e., it is deposited in the bone. This isotope completely destroys the bone marrow by virtue of its bone-seeking property and its emission of radiation, because the isotope is localized in close proximity to the site of blood cell formation. The radioactive decay of the 89-strontium results in eradication of the cellular elements of the marrow. Even though the animal is devoid of functional bone marrow, it does not become anemic. As was the case with estradiol, the spleen takes over the function of blood cell formation. The question then became "how did the spleen 'know' that the marrow was no longer producing blood cells and that it had to become the principal source of them?" This question became the central theme of a great deal of research in Jake's lab over a number of years and eventually a satisfactory, but partial, answer emerged.

In the late 1940s and early 50s, in still another approach to the problem, he used total body X-irradiation to completely destroy the bone marrow cells. Before the mice were placed in the x-ray beam, however, their spleens were exteriorized and placed in small lead boxes to shield them from the radiation. The blood supply to and from the spleen was left intact, and after an otherwise lethal dose of radiation the spleens were replaced in the mice. More than 70% of the mice with shielded spleens survived the large dose of x-rays, while of the non-shielded mice less than 1% survived. This surprising result was made even more surprising by subsequent experiments. If the shielded spleen was removed surgically rather than returned to the body after the radiation dose, the mice survived equally well. Even if the interval between the radiation and the discarding of the shielded spleen were as short as five minutes, there was a significant number of mice that survived the radiation. These experiments were followed by others in which bits of intact splenic tissue were implanted into previously radiated mice, again with the result that the mice survived. In still further experiments, spleen or bone marrow cells injected into the blood stream of mice after total body radiation, without spleen shielding, also resulted in significant survival of the radiated mice. In still further experiments, bone marrow cells from species other than mice (e.g., rabbit or rat) were given to irradiated mice. Those cells were also effective to some extent in preventing radiation death.

All of these findings demonstrated that, in mice, some property of the spleen was fully capable of maintaining blood cell formation in the absence of functioning marrow, and that death due to radiation could be avoided if the spleen or some splenic tissue was spared. Jake, commenting on this work, once wrote that "To my knowledge, this was the first time that anyone had saved the life of a lethally irradiated animal."

The fact that the shielded spleen had an effect in protecting against radiation death even after a short period of time, and the cross-species effect, led Jake to the potentially important hypothesis that survival after lethal amounts of radiation might be effected by a substance or group of substances coming from the spleen—the humoral hypothesis. The crux of this hypothesis was that non-irradiated spleen (or marrow or liver) cells produced something, whether while in the lead shield, in the peritoneum, or elsewhere in the body and this something "cured" the radiation injury. The cross-species results appeared to lend important support to the hypothesis, since it was assumed that cells of non-mouse origin could not survive in the recipient irradiated mice.

To quote Jake on the humoral hypothesis:

> In view of these observations, it seems extremely unlikely that cell migration from the shielded or transplanted tissue and subsequent proliferation of these cells account for the reconstitution of hematopoietic tissues and increased survival of irradiated animals, or that neutralization of some "toxins" produced by irradiation can account for these findings. Perhaps neither of these possibilities can be positively excluded on the basis of the evidence presented, but the evidence strongly suggests that the factor (or factors) responsible for recovery from radiation under these circumstances is non-cellular and may be required only for the initiation of the repair process. The factor (or factors) may be quite labile or, as is more likely, may be produced in an effective quantity only by living cells.

The humoral hypothesis, if verified, could have had a striking impact, especially during that period of heightened fear of nuclear attack during the Cold War. It was an era (1950s) when school children were taught to hide under their classroom desks for protection in the event of a nuclear bombing. If radiation injury could be "cured" by administration of a "substance," perhaps derived from slaughterhouse spleens, that portion of the general population not killed outright by the blast or heat could be spared the devastation due to radiation sickness resulting after an attack with nuclear weapons. It seemed to be important that the humoral hypothesis be studied as quickly and intensively as possible. It was surprising, but fortunate, considering the later findings, that a nationwide, large-scale project to exploit this possible anti-radiation therapy was never established.

The focal question related to the humoral hypothesis was whether the observed effect was due to cells or to the postulated non-cellular spleen factor. If the latter were true, it would be possible, in principle, to isolate, characterize, and perhaps synthesize it for use as an anti-radiation drug.

An amusing sideline to a serious problem: Jake invited Leo Szilard, the eminent physicist, to meet with him and me to discuss the spleen factor question on a Saturday afternoon at the lab. The great physicist had not known of Jake's experiments but was very much interested in the problem due to his concern about nuclear war and to his new career in biology. After the end of WWII, he had given up working in physics because of constraints due to secrecy and instead devoted himself to biological problems. After listening to Jake explain the spleen shielding results, he proposed an ingenious experiment to determine whether it was cells or some non-cellular substance that initiated the recovery from radiation damage. It was an elegant idea but would have been very difficult to work on experimentally. Being young and, I guess, callow, I said something like "Now why couldn't I have thought of that?" Szilard answered, "That's the difference between genius and fools." At any rate, the method Szilard proposed would have involved an immense amount of work and was, however brilliant, extremely risky. Other ideas, easier to implement, were needed.

All of us associated with Jake's lab, however, lost sight of an important finding, first reported in 1915, that radiation destroyed the body's ability to mount an immune response to foreign material. Had Jake given that observation the weight it warranted, the idea that the cross-species effect meant that cells were not involved would no longer be a cogent argument. The foreign cells could have repopulated the radiated mouse, providing a new blood-forming system, characteristic of the donor and sparing the life of the recipient, for a while, in the case of cells of non-mouse origin. Later, these cells, of non-mouse origin, would produce, in the recipient mice, cells capable of their own immune response which would recognize the recipient mice as foreign and produce antibodies against the host mice. This is the "graft vs. host" response. Because of the fixation on the humoral hypothesis and its great potential benefits, too little attention was paid to the alternative view.

We had planned an experiment that involved labeling the DNA of the donor spleen cells with a radioactive tracer and then examining the unlabeled, irradiated recipient mice for cells with radioactivity derived from the donor cells. As we were in the first stages of this experiment, the group of investigators at Harwell (the British research station associated with their atomic energy program) solved the problem and published their results in 1956. They showed very convincingly, by an elegant approach using marked chromosomes that could be distinguished from the host cells, that the blood-forming system of the radiated mouse, protected by injection of normal marrow cells, was repopulated by donor mouse cells. The chromosomes of the recipient mice were not present in the blood-forming system of rescued animals, but those of the donor mice were. Three years earlier, in July of 1953, Jake had written to John Loutit, who headed the Harwell group, that "My work hasn't progressed very far beyond where it was a year or more ago. We (are) still hoping that one day we'll come through with the isolation of (the) elusive substance or substances in the spleen and marrow which affects survival of irradiated mice." A year before that he had written to Egon Lorenz at the National Institutes of Health, with whom he collaborated on marrow cell injection experiments, that he was ". . . continuing to have negative results from the injection of cell-free preparations, but haven't given up hope yet. I am expecting that one morning I shall wake up with the alarm clock and suddenly get the idea which will solve the problem. When I do I'll call you immediately." He clearly had a major scientific and emotional investment in the idea that there was a curative substance involved. Jake's optimism may have been due, in part, to a phone message from a Dr. Porsche of the Armour Research Laboratory, on a closely related subject. In 1949, or earlier, Porsche reported that he had made rabbits severely deficient in white blood cells by administration of benzene. Such animals then treated with an extract of yellow bone marrow [yellow marrow contains mostly fat rather than blood cell precursors] showed an almost complete recovery. This was looked on as a model of radiation injury and treatment. No further mention of this experiment is to be found in the literature or in the collected papers.

 The humoral hypothesis was too attractive to discard easily, even in the face of evidence that tended to weaken it significantly. Many advances in science have been based on ideas that were not accepted at the time they were proposed and that appeared to be falsified by the then available data. It takes time for the reconciliation of a correct concept with apparently contradictory evidence, but it has happened. Discarding a concept when the contrary evidence is less than compelling can be an impediment to progress in science, especially if the discarded hypothesis has important ramifications. One example, that of Darwin's hypothesis that the evolution of species proceeded through natural selection, should suffice to make the point.

 Jake's humoral hypothesis seemed to be important enough to follow until the contrary data were sufficiently persuasive to force its abandonment. The Harwell group provided that persuasion. In addition, there was so much national publicity in newspapers and on the radio about the "substance" that could cure radiation sickness that Jake may have been victim of his own press conferences. For instance, an April 2, 1957, press release read: "The life saving substance in spleen is some sort of secretion, possible a hormone, rather than the spleen itself. The studies indicate that it may be possible in the future, to pre-treat some types of cancer patients with anti-radiation prophylactics, and then give them greater than usual X-ray doses." This, of course, is the converse of the successful method used by Thomas, who treated the cancers with X-rays and then rescued the patients with bone marrow cells. Among the spate of publicity, there was an article in the *Chicago Daily News* on December 12, 1951, that listed the "anti-radiation factor" as one of the ten top "gains" of that year. In the *Chicago Sun Times* of November 24, 1952, Jake is quoted as follows: "Identification of this substance is not yet complete. But progress is always rapid when a problem of national importance is valued and it can be said clues to the solution are at hand." Later that year the *Chicago Tribune* ran an editorial saying, "Dr. Jacobson has, what he considers, a cure of a most threatening malady, the effects of atomic radiation."

Another facet of the reluctance to accept the cell re-population alternative to the humoral hypothesis was due to the more-or-less unsophisticated state of knowledge about the stem cells that are the precursors of blood cells. The last 15 to 20 years of research has made it clear, without contradiction, that there is a single class of cells capable of being the progenitor of all of the types of circulating blood cells. In the early 1950s, when Jake did his spleen-shielding experiments, the question of whether there was indeed such a thing as a single stem cell, or whether there might be several types of stem cells, each the source of one type of blood cell, was still being debated.

With hindsight it is clear that the results of Jake's experiments can all be explained by the transfer of stem cells either from the shielded spleen, or contained in bits of implanted tissue or from spleen or marrow cells injected into the circulation. Those stem cells, contained in the mixture of exogenous spleen or marrow cells, then find a "home" in the bone cavity among the cells killed by the radiation, and grow to repopulate the blood-forming system, sparing the life of the radiated mouse. Jake's spleen-shielding experiments are now recognized as the first to show the existence of stem cells in circulating blood.

Had Jake pursued the possibility that cellular re-population was the mechanism of the shielded-spleen effect, because of his clinical background and early interest in diseases of the blood-forming system and in radiation therapy he might well have extended his ideas to the subject of such therapy for various cancers. In this approach, the cancer would be eliminated by total body irradiation followed by transplantation of intact normal human bone marrow cells to rescue the patient.

Don Thomas in Seattle did just that and received the Nobel Prize in Medicine and Physiology for showing that tumors of various kinds could be eradicated by radiation of the patient followed by transplantation of intact bone marrow cells to repopulate the blood-forming system. If the transplanted cells were not identical to those of the patient, they would eventually reconstitute a foreign immune system that would recognize the recipient patient as non-self and produce a devastating immune response against the patient. For this reason, careful matching of donor and patient has to be done and patients have to be treated with drugs to minimize the immune response.

Jake was considerably miffed that the Nobel committee did not award him a share of the prize, because his work did provide the original basis for clinically successful bone marrow transplantation. In a lecture at the University of Chicago, Don Thomas acknowledged that his work on bone marrow transplantation was built on the observations that Jake made. The siren song of the potential of the humoral hypothesis was just too strong to resist and Jake may have envisioned himself in the company of Jenner, Pasteur, and Salk as major benefactors of humanity. He just bet on the wrong horse.

CHAPTER SEVEN

Argonne Cancer Research Hospital

". . . can someone please say something good about the Chicago White Sox?"

By the end of World War II, Jake had made many contacts and friends among the university and Federal administrators, especially those in the medical sciences, and was recognized as a potential star in academic medicine. His success administering the health section of the Metallurgical Lab project was appreciated widely. In 1945, a new dean, R. Wendall Harrison, was appointed to replace William H. Taliaferro. He quickly learned of Jake's abilities and appointed him as an Associate Dean in the Division of Biological Sciences while he was still an Assistant Professor in the Department of Medicine. The new chairman of Medicine, Dr. Lowell T. Coggeshall, generally known as Cog, soon replaced Harrison as Dean. He and Jake became close friends and he asked Jake to prepare a plan for the University and the Division of Biological Sciences to take advantage of the new interest in, and support of, research by the Federal government. This was partly a result of the great success of the Manhattan Project. Cog was interested in applying the Metallurgical Lab expertise, in all its forms, to medical research and that too was part of the charge Jake got for the plan.

There was, at about the same time, a significant degree of disgruntlement on the part of the Manhattan Project scientists who were unhappy about the arbitrary restrictions imposed on them and their work by the military administration. One typical instance that was reported was that at a conference of the senior research staff in Chicago, General Leslie Groves, who was the overall head of the project, interrupted their discussion and threatened to ship them all off to Guadalcanal in the Pacific. Also at about this time, at some levels of the federal government, there were plans to establish several National Laboratories that were to concentrate on large-scale projects in physics, chemistry, and radiation biology that might be too big for the usual university setting. Among these plans was one for the Argonne National Lab, to be administered by the University of Chicago and to be built in a forest preserve some thirty miles from the campus. There was also lively discussion on the national scene about control of the atomic energy program. Some strong voices in favor of military control were opposed by equally strong voices for civilian control. Robert M. Hutchins, President of the University of Chicago was among those who were in favor of civilian control. Civilian control won out and the Atomic Energy Commission was established.

Hutchins was also trying to keep at the University of Chicago some of the major scientists who had been recruited to the Metallurgical Lab from other institutions. To this end, Arthur H. Compton, Nobel Laureate in Physics and head of the Metallurgical Lab as well as Dean of Physical Sciences, offered Enrico Fermi a position on the Physics faculty. Isidore Rabi, at Columbia, where Fermi still had an appointment, was angry about this attempt at a raid and turned to Vannevar Bush, who was the head of the National Defense Research Council to help prevent the attempted piracy. Bush informed Compton that if the University of Chicago went ahead with the ploy, he would act to have Argonne National Lab taken out of the University of Chicago's domain. Compton thought it was a bluff. He was right and the University stayed as primary contractor for Argonne Lab. He renewed the offer to Fermi along with five other physicists; they accepted and the University of Chicago started to organize an Institute of Nuclear Studies around Fermi and his group. It featured the cyclotron the University had built before the war with private funds.

While all this was going on, Cog had started the University of Chicago Cancer Research Foundation to raise funds for research including application of high-energy physics for treatment of cancers and the use of radio-isotopes for therapeutic and investigational purposes. There was, in addition, a plan to raise funds for a new, larger cyclotron to be used for both high-energy physics research and by the radiologists for treatment of cancers. The Office of Naval Research was asked to provide half of the needed funding and the University planned to raise 9 million dollars, including 3.1 million dollars for the building and equipment. The physicists were leery of the arrangement, thinking that use of the resources for clinical purposes would encroach on the time they would have for their research. There was, inevitably, much friction and change of plans.

The plan Jake delivered to Cog envisioned a hospital with a modest number of "research" beds and extensive research laboratories, as well as high-energy instrumentation for treatment of cancers and facilities for use of radio-isotopes for both diagnosis and treatment. Cog, now Dean of the Division, was much taken with Jake's plan and in spite of other priorities decided to act immediately. Federal research funding had been specifically directed away from building at teaching institutions, but some money was available for renovation of existing laboratories, and Cog quickly called his friend Leonard Scheele, the Surgeon General of the United States, who had the responsibility for distribution of funds for research on diseases. Scheele urged Cog to apply but indicated that eligibility was dubious because the money available through his office was restricted to heart disease and cancer. A hospital centered on the use of radioactivity would probably not qualify. Jake and Cog decided to call it the Cancer Isotope Hospital at the University of Chicago. Their plan was estimated to cost about three million dollars, of which the University administration and trustees would supply half. Scheele thought the remaining 1.5 million dollars was too much for his budget, but offered to determine whether the newly formed Atomic Energy Commission (AEC) would be willing to collaborate.

In mid-1947, the AEC officially announced that it was not interested in either cancer research or in cancer treatment. Jake and Cog, having been rebuffed by the AEC, went to the National Cancer Institute (NCI) for funding, aided by Cog's contacts at the National Institutes of Health. NCI indicated that any grants it might make were most likely to be far smaller than the University was planning for.

While Cog and Jake were scrambling to find funding for their project, the then chairman of the Senate committee on atomic energy, Sen. Brian McMahon, died of cancer, followed shortly thereafter by the death of Sen. Arthur Vandenberg, a senior member of the Senate Foreign Relations Committee, of the same disease. The members of Congress quickly passed legislation directing the AEC to become involved in cancer research.

The commission now had to find "cancer" projects to support by April 20, 1947. L. Straus, one of the commissioners, presented a budget to a House committee with no funds for research on cancer or for therapy using radioactivity. Twenty days later, Sen. Everett Dirksen of Illinois spoke about spending "a little" of the $250–300 million AEC appropriation to save the lives of cancer patients, who were dying at a yearly rate 72 times greater than the number of casualties at Pearl Harbor. He proposed to set aside $25 million of the AEC budget to be used exclusively for cancer research. His proposal quickly won Senate approval. The AEC was blindsided by the Senate and the commission did not like the whole idea. The chairman, David Lilienthal, considered that the AEC already had too big a job and shouldn't also take on cancer research. The Senate bill directed the AEC to "make available for cancer research such amounts it believed can be used well." The Senate-House conference committee reduced the $25 million to $5 million and the commission allocated the funds for (1) studies of the effects of radiation on cancers developed by the survivors of the nuclear bomb attacks on Hiroshima and Nagasaki; (2) providing free isotopes from the reactors at the national labs, especially Oak Ridge National Lab, for research and treatment; (3) contracts concerning cancer research; and (4) building small cancer research facilities at each of the national labs.

As of the middle of 1948, the AEC was able to figure out how to spend only $1.3 million, but the money had to be obligated by June 30, the end of the fiscal year. Jake and Cog had submitted a plan to the AEC for an "isotope hospital" to be built not at Argonne National Lab but on the University of Chicago campus. There was no major objection because the Argonne National Lab administration did not want a cancer hospital at their facility. Since the AEC had indicated that the cancer research funded by them was to be done at a National Lab, the "isotope hospital" was called the Argonne Cancer Research Hospital to suggest that it was part of Argonne National Lab. It was, but in a very loose administrative manner. On June 28, two days before the deadline, the AEC delivered a letter with the contract for construction of the building at a cost of $3.5 million and $1.5 million for equipping the hospital, along with $1.1 million for the first year of operation. The University executed the contract on June 29. It is not clear how the $6.1 million was derived from the $3.7 million presumably left from the original $5 million.

Argonne Cancer Research Hospital (ACRH) was officially opened in 1953 as part of the University of Chicago medical complex, with Jake as its Director. It cost $2.72 million to build but it is not known whether the saved money went back to the AEC. In keeping with the original plan that Jake formulated, ACRH was a six-story building above ground and two stories below ground. The sub-basement housed three high-energy instruments for the potential treatment of cancers. One was a very potent radioactive cobalt source housed in a shield made of depleted uranium that could be mechanically rotated around the patient, with the gamma-ray radiation focused at the point of the tumor, sparing the non-tumor tissue from most of the radiation. Another rotational therapy instrument involved a Van der Graff generator, which could irradiate tumors with x-rays or high-energy electrons. The third machine was a linear accelerator, using even higher-energy electrons. All three were state of the art for that time.

Nearby were enormous glass-lined tanks to retain radioactive waste from the whole building and store it until it decayed enough to make it safe to be disposed of through the city sewage system, or, if a sufficient amount of time for decay was not allowed, to be transferred to trucks and taken to Argonne National Lab for whatever method they chose for disposal.

The basement held an "isotope pharmacy" where very radioactive materials were prepared for administration to patients in the clinical section of ACRH. Much of the preparation involved remote control arms operated from the outside of a heavily shielded "cave." There were also some research labs in the basement. The ground floor contained administrative offices, a conference room, and superbly equipped machine and electronics shops for designing and building specialized equipment for the research labs and therapeutic facilities.

The second floor contained Jake's office and his small lab as well as labs and offices for some of the scientific staff. Jake's two co-workers, Edna Marks and Evelyn Gaston, were devoted recorder and flute players and every day after they finished their brown-bag lunches the whole second floor of ACRH was treated to their enchanting music.

The third and fourth floors contained rooms for patients who were parts of studies, being treated with isotopes or the high-energy sources. At Jake's insistence, these patients were not charged for their hospital stays. Jake made the point that they were research patients who were being studied with respect to new approaches to possible cancer treatment. The fifth floor was, again, labs and offices, while the sixth floor was a small-animal farm providing mice, rats, and rabbits for all of the research groups. It also housed a facility for diagnostic radiation and for radiating animals for experimental purposes, as well as Dr. Simmons's research lab.

The building was designed to be the last word with respect to safe use of radioactivity for research and therapy. Each room in ACRH was to be kept at a lower pressure than the hallway, so that any leak of radioactivity would be swept out by air flow from the hall and out the ventilation system, which was filtered. The labs all had pressure monitors that would sound alarms when the pressure rose above a pre-set level, signaling the danger of contaminated air getting out. The settings of these alarms were such that there was frequent bell ringing, so frequent that we all learned quickly how to defeat the alarm, making possible some danger but letting us retain our sanity. In the design of the building, the architects put the air intake for the whole hospital at ground level, very close to the loading dock where trucks with idling engines poured out exhaust fumes that were then quickly swept into the air intake. Even though the air was filtered and cleaned, when a delivery was made the exhaust fumes were taken into the intake system and then made their way to the first and second floors. They finally had to put a large plywood baffle in place to keep the fumes out. When asked why the air intake was not put on the roof, six floors up, the university architect said it would have "marred the roofline."

ARCH operated under an "umbrella" contract. There was an annual budget from the AEC, which was allocated among the various sub-projects by negotiation between Jake, the project leader, and the AEC. Some research expenses, such as animals, isotopes, and machine shop costs, were subsumed in their own separate budgets and essentially did not cost the investigators anything. Jake had a great deal of flexibility in budgeting and could expand or contract existing projects or initiate new ones with little interference from the AEC. He could allocate funds where he thought they could be used most effectively.

One example of how this ability to seize the day can be seen in the career of Dr. Janet Rowley. She came back to the University of Chicago after a time in Oxford, where her husband, who was a professor of Pathology, was on sabbatical in the Dunn School of Pathology. While in Oxford, she started to work on cytogenetics, the study of chromosomes in disease states. Back in Chicago, she asked Jake for some space, the use of a good microscope, and a very modest budget. He recognized her ability and the potential of her proposal and helped her get started in ACRH. Within a short time, she became one of the world's leading authorities on the role of chromosome changes in the diseases of the blood-forming system.

The federal office kept a moderately close watch on the number, quality, and relevance of the several sub-projects, although Jake's personality generally dominated high-level discussions about ACRH.

I was once visited by a member of the AEC staff who wanted to know in some detail what I was doing, why, and how I handled my modest budget. I thought little about this visit until I learned that he had not interviewed other project leaders and I, of course, worried about why I had been singled out. A year later, he was back asking me the same questions. I then asked him why he spent time with me when my small lab was such a minor part of the ACRH operation in contrast with the big-ticket high-energy labs. He told me that before his previous visit he had been at a Congressional budget hearing for the AEC and someone opened a big book, ran his finger down the page, stopped, and asked one of the commissioners about this person in Chicago named Goldwasser; what was he doing? The commissioner, who probably had never heard my name before, turned to his associate to answer the question. He didn't know much more but somehow stumbled through an explanation of my work and then made a promise to himself never to go to a Congressional budget hearing without first coming to see what I was up to.

There was a meeting of the project leaders every week, which Jake usually opened with a joke or story and was characterized by great informality, and little of substance. The research staff was composed, in the main, of members of the academic departments: Medicine, Surgery, Physics, Radiology, Biochemistry, Pharmacology, and Chemistry. Jake made most of the decisions by himself, with only occasional input from others. One aspect of his seat-of-the-pants administration arose near the end of every fiscal year, when word would come to project leaders that there was an urgent need to spend money. If spending was significantly lower than budgeted, the next year's budget would be cut. Jake routinely kept spending down during the year to be sure that he did not run short of funds. We then had to make a great effort to spend whatever funds were still available.

As administrator of ACRH, Jake showed his great ability at dealing with small groups. The availability of funds and the informality of the weekly meetings led to humor and collegiality among the staff, with very little of the contentiousness frequently found in academic groups. For a number of years, ACRH was truly an investigator's dream of scientific paradise come true. It took very little time to write proposals or attend meetings. The immense advantage of being able to get funding for new departures in research, or for expanding a promising line of study without a major effort to convince an official of a governmental agency, was evident. This situation, made possible by Jake, allowed him to take advantage of unexpected opportunities, which he did quite successfully.

For the most part, Jake chose well when staffing ACRH, but in some cases he relied on friendship in making appointments and some of those were not successful. He nevertheless remained loyal to his friends and preferred to let them ease themselves out rather than do it himself.

After some years, the AEC was dissolved and succeeded by an agency called ERDA, which in turn was succeeded by the Department of Energy. During these administrative changes, the confusion between ACRH and Argonne National Lab was finally put to rest when the former became The Franklin McLean Research Institute, named after one of the founding faculty members of the University of Chicago medical school. McLean was an eminent physiologist who had been director of the Toxicity Lab early on.

When Jake became chairman of Medicine, he resigned the directorship of ACRH in favor of Dr. Alexander Gottschalk, a radiologist who was also on the ACRH staff. Jake later realized that the appointment was, to put it mildly, an unfortunate mistake. When he became Dean of the Division, the mild-mannered Jake, who almost always avoided confrontation, was engaged in a hallway shouting match with Gottschalk. He then convinced Gottschalk to leave Chicago and put himself back into the directorship. By this time, the new emphasis in the mission of the Department of Energy changed the entire thrust of the research in ACRH and made the Institute a very different place. The shift away from Biology and Medicine to environmental problems essentially eliminated most of the existing ACRH programs. Jake's dream institute became a very ordinary part of the hospital complex.

Jake was powerless to influence the course of events and had to watch his creation disappear.

During most of its life, ACRH was visited very often by delegations from all over the world, including the Soviet Union and China, to learn about this innovation in research and treatment of cancer. In November of 1958, five years after the opening of the world's first "atomic" hospital, Queen Frederika of Greece paid a formal state visit, with Jake as host. He had been instructed by the consular staff that the elevators had to be emptied so that no one could accidentally touch her. In the cobalt therapy facility, a press photographer who called her "Queenie," took her arm to position her for a photograph. She was furious and had him ejected from the room.

One such visit was by a group from South America, and at the customary dinner for the visiting dignitaries with the ACRH staff, there was speech after speech by one after the other of the visitors, all of them saying essentially the same things—in praise of the hospital, of Jake, of the University, and of the U.S. government. This went on for so long that many of us, having drunk deeply of the free-flowing wine, began to nod off or make snide comments to each other about the speeches. As our eyes glazed over, Jake finally rose to his feet and in response to the guest's comments said something along these lines: "There has been much said in glowing terms about our institution; now can someone please say something good about the Chicago White Sox?" He then sat down and the speech making ended.

Jake with Queen Frederika of Greece during her visit to the Argonne Cancer Research Hospital in 1958. Paul V. Harper, Associate Director of the hospital in the background.

CHAPTER EIGHT

Erythropoietin

"How does the spleen of a mouse know that it should start to produce blood cells?"

Given his long-term, deep fascination with the biology of blood cell formation and the recovery of the blood-forming system from radiation injury, it was almost inevitable that Jake would turn to the study of erythropoietin (epo). Although the science of blood cell formation and of its control by epo is not a topic of this book, a brief background might help some readers understand Jake's approach to another important problem in medical science.

In mammals, the total amount of circulating red blood cells, the erythron, is held relatively constant under normal circumstances. In humans, red cells are formed normally at a rate of about 2.5 million per second unless some perturbation occurs. It had been known for a long time that significant loss of red cells—for example, by bleeding—would be compensated by accelerated formation of new red cells until the original level was regained. It was also known that if the amount of oxygen in the inhaled air were reduced—for example, by going to a high altitude, thus diminishing oxygen delivery to the tissues—a mechanism was put in place to increase the size of the erythron, in order to deliver sufficient oxygen to permit normal tissue function. For a long while, the general opinion of those interested in the question was that the bone marrow, where red cells are formed, somehow sensed the oxygen deficit and corrected it by making more red cells.

The understanding of the mechanism of regulation of erythron size took on a new dimension in 1906 when a paper by Paul Carnot and Camille Deflandre was published in France. In this paper, the authors claimed to have demonstrated that there was a substance appearing in the circulation of rabbits after they were bled, a considerable amount, that could stimulate the formation of new red cells. They called this putative substance "hemopoietine." The basic idea proposed by the French investigators was what we would now call a feedback mechanism: when red cells are needed hemopoietine is made; it then acts to increase the number of red cells and when the "set point" is once again reached the stimulation ceases.

The major trouble with this concept was that the reported experimental results could not be confirmed by others, despite many attempts by many people over many years to do so. It took about 40 years before other sorts of experiments did confirm the basic idea. By the mid-1950s, the existence of such a substance, now called erythropoietin (known familiarly as epo) was established.

Jake started to think seriously about epo when he was still in thrall to the non-cellular radiation recovery factor. Epo might be part of his postulated mechanism since it was a circulating substance and had an effect on the blood-forming system. Jake also connected the existence of epo with the question that had tantalized him for some years: how does the spleen of a mouse "know" that it should start to produce blood cells when the bone marrow was not functioning? The answer could involve epo, although there must be other important factors involving white blood cell formation, which were the more important aspects of the radiation experiments. Epo has no effect on white blood cell formation, but there is evidence of other factors that could be involved in a manner analogous to the action of epo on red cell formation.

In ACRH, Jake had a very modest lab with his two technicians who had worked with him since the Metallurgical Lab days: Edna Marks and Evelyn Gaston. These two played a vital role in all of Jake's research, but he needed more hands and more brains for the new project he had in mind, and recruited two medical students, Walter Fried and Louis Plzak, to work with him. This kind of collaboration with medical students was one aspect of Jake's devotion to teaching. He actively looked for ways to get students involved in serious research, finding funds for them and shielding them from other drains on their time. Along with the students he also relied on faculty colleagues for technical advice.

The immediate objective was to devise a reliable method for measuring epo. Previous work on epo used assay methods that were not quantitative and could yield, at best, only yes-or-no answers. Jake then asked Drs. William Bethard and Kiku Nakao, a visiting professor from Tokyo University, to help out with the quantitative aspects of the method they were developing. Somewhat later he asked me to join the team and as I got more deeply into the problem, he seduced me into working on epo almost full time. My task, in addition to making the assay quantitative was to purify and characterize epo, as well as to oversee the students' experiments. The problem was so challenging it became my main research effort. What I, at first, thought would be a 6–12 month time out from my other research turned out to take about 20 years.

Jake, the students, and I collaborated on a number of topics that could be done without the need for pure epo. Most of the ideas in this phase of our work originated with Jake due to his deep knowledge of medicine and biology, coupled with his intuitive approach to problem solving. The contributions of the students, however, should not be minimized. The four of us met regularly to discuss results, to parcel out writing chores for the papers we were publishing, and to plan further experiments.

One recurrent subject of discussion centered about the obvious question of where in the body epo was made. This was a time of major interest in pituitary hormones and it seemed that epo could well be a pituitary hormone. Rats without pituitary glands become anemic and preparations containing epo could correct the anemia. Superficially, such evidence could be considered to demonstrate the pituitary source of epo. Using rats that had had their pituitary glands removed and then made anemic and showing that they still made epo after blood loss, pretty much made the pituitary source untenable. In one meeting on the subject, Jake told us he knew where epo was made and wrote it on a piece of paper that he then sealed in an envelope and gave to his secretary to hold until we had finished the experiments.

When our first results were in, largely due to Fried and Plzak, we brought them to Jake, who then produced the piece of paper with his prediction on it. He had gotten it right; our results showed that epo was produced in the kidneys of rats. It was never clear how he had arrived at the right answer, but his vast clinical experience probably led him to it. He knew, for instance, that patients with chronic kidney disease were anemic, but that by itself would not be sufficient evidence for the conclusion.

When our paper on the kidney as the source of epo was accepted by a journal, Jake called a press conference to announce the finding. The ACRH conference room was set up for reporters and photographers, with coffee and pastries available. Nobody came. Jake was crestfallen, but got over it with a joke.

Our experimental evidence was rather soft and might be interpreted to yield several different conclusions, so we had to do more, and more rigorous, experiments to answer the various objections. One colleague, at a national meeting, commented as follows: A man trained a flea to jump on the command "jump." He then removed one leg, issued the command, and the flea obeyed. He then proceeded to remove one leg at a time and told the flea to jump, and the flea did until, the sixth and last leg was gone and the flea did not jump. Conclusion: fleas hear with their legs. Clearly, removal of the kidneys is a very severe insult to an animal and will perturb many functions, some of which could then, in a secondary manner, interfere with epo production by some organ other than the kidney. Before too long, however, the consensus based on results from several labs was that epo was a kidney hormone, even though the evidence was still not conclusive. It took almost 30 years, until the advent of molecular biology, before we could produce the hard, conclusive evidence needed.

Following up on our paper on the kidney, there was an important confirmatory paper published in Poland by Zofia Kuratowska and her colleagues in Warsaw. A few years later, Kuratowska came to the University of Chicago to work with Jake. He hated to not accept people who wanted to be part of his lab team and frequently accepted them when he was far too busy to guide their research. He then would ask either Clifford Gurney or me to take them on. Kuratowska worked in my lab and while she was there left her purse on top of her desk when she went to a lecture. Her purse was rifled and $80 was stolen. Because she was Polish and the Cold War was on, she could not be supported on ACRH funds and so lived on a limited amount of money that her father, Kasimir Kuratowski, an eminent mathematician, had accumulated in a U.S. bank account. The loss of $80 was important to her and Jake, realizing the spot it put her in, gave her a personal check for the amount. He then put in a request for reimbursement from some non-governmental fund he had. In his written request, he said not to worry if it couldn't be done because he had a part-time job shoveling snow off his neighbors' sidewalks. He was paid 80 cents a week, so in 100 weeks he'd be solvent again.

Edna Marks and Jake placing a mouse spleen into a lead box in their search for the hypothetical radiation recovery factor.

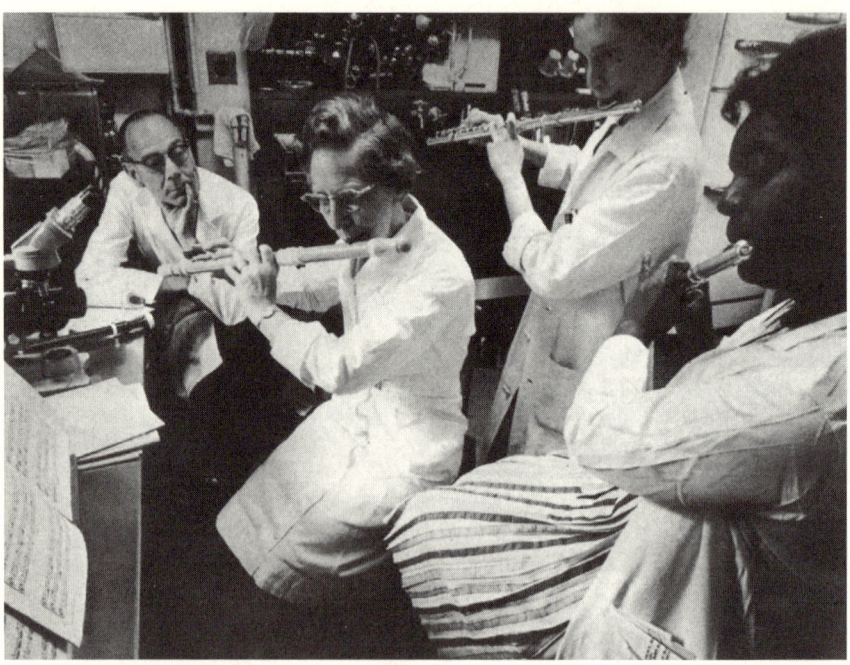

Jake, Edna Marks, Sherry Steinberg (student), and Evelyn Gaston during a noontime concert on the second floor of the Argonne Cancer Research Hospital.

Accepting that epo was a kidney hormone and that patients with kidney disease who were on dialysis were anemic due to lack of epo, and needed blood transfusions periodically, made it clear that there was an important possible clinical use for epo if it could ever be obtained pure and in a large enough quantity. The lack of epo in the serum of patients with kidney disease was an assumption based on inferences but not on measurements, because at that time there was no method sensitive enough to measure epo in the circulation of those patients. It took a few years before we could measure it, and we did, in fact, find the presumed low level of epo in their plasma.

When we started on the epo project, Jake assured me that his two technicians would supply all the plasma from anemic animals that I might need for purification of epo, and that the two students would do all the assays I might need. It seemed like a good arrangement and I accepted it without questioning it or even thinking hard about it. Within a short time, it became abundantly clear how unrealistic the plan was. I really could not rely on the students, who had medical school classes to worry about, to do all the assays I needed, when I needed them. Once I started on the purification task, it was equally clear that Edna Marks and Evelyn Gaston would not be able to supply me with enough starting material. One early experiment showed that even in rabbit plasma from very severely anemic animals, epo was present as an extremely minute component. The most that could be obtained from rabbits was orders of magnitude lower than we needed, and a very much larger source was required. I then had to organize my own lab to take over the assays and to find another source of epo. Jake was highly supportive of my lab with funds, space, and personnel. As far as the purification aspect of the project was concerned, however, Jake was kept informed but was no longer an integral part since he realized it was the kind of science he knew little about.

He took the initiative in the supply problem, using his contacts both in the National Institutes of Health and at Armour and Company, which had a research unit near Chicago that was involved with large-scale production of pituitary hormones. The Armour lab agreed to explore the possibility of producing epo from anemic sheep. Jake then got a contract from NIH, with me as co-investigator and Armour as collaborator, to produce a large amount of pure sheep epo for use by the scientific community. Sheep were chosen because they were available in large numbers near the Armour experimental farm. They were so-called cull breeder sheep, of no agricultural value except as a source of pet food.

Under the NIH contract, Armour bought the sheep, made them anemic, and harvested the plasma. Their lab and mine then worked together to develop methods to purify the plasma epo. My lab did all the assays to monitor progress in purification. Usually in my lab we would do a small-scale purification experiment, which would then be scaled up by the Armour lab. The partially purified epo was then delivered to my lab to be held pending NIH decisions about its distribution. A committee was set up by NIH to solicit requests for the available epo and to allocate the epo. I would then be told which lab was to get how much of the partially purified sheep epo, and I would send it out.

This method of distribution was based on both our original proposal to NIH and the intention of the review panel that approved it. Their intent was to expedite research on epo by providing scarce materials to interested investigators. It served that purpose well but since only one or two labs were engaged in, or capable of, studies of purification and since the bulk of the sheep epo was used for other purposes, the distribution method, in fact, decreased the pace of purification work beyond what could have been accomplished had a much larger portion of the available epo been used for purification. The allocation I received was mostly side-fractions that were less pure than that sent to the other labs, but in a much greater amount. We did finally get what we thought was pure sheep epo: it required a purification of one million fold over the starting material. The final product amounted to 200 micrograms (7 millionth of an ounce) and was far too little for chemical characterization or for any clinical use. There was, however, a clinical experiment done in a lab at the university using quite impure sheep plasma epo on a normal volunteer, a member of the lab group. This trial, which would never be approved by any committee now, showed only that the epo used was too impure, toxic, and dangerous for human use. Fortunately, there was no lasting effect on the volunteer.

The NIH panel decided that the sheep program was not a feasible way to go about obtaining epo and did not renew the contract. To Jake and me, it looked as though epo was fated to remain an intriguing biological curiosity. The prospects for future epo research looked grim indeed. Jake's dream of doing a clinical trial with epo dimmed greatly, since the resources at his disposal were much too limited to be able to go on with the sheep project, and the prospect of getting any pure human epo looked even less likely.

One fall-out of the epo program, however, was a partial answer to his question about how the spleen "knew" it had to make blood cells. When red cells are lacking, the reduced delivery of oxygen to the kidneys stimulates that organ to secrete more epo than usual, informing the spleen of the task ahead. That answer is partial, because the spleen also makes white blood cells, which are more important in the recovery from radiation injury. Although it has not yet been completely established, the same sort of picture is probably true for white blood cell formation, in responding to some factors analogous to epo.

Jake lived to see epo become the most successful product of the newly established bio-tech industry. The years of his retirement saw the purification of human epo, the determination of its sequence, the cloning of its gene, the expression of human epo in an industrial amount, and the success of the clinical trials showing that anemic patients on dialysis and patients with anemias due to treatment of cancer with chemotherapy could be freed of the need for transfusions. All of this was the result of his foresight in starting to study epo back in the early 1950s when the "smart money" said it was a fool's game. Jake would have been impressed by the fact that epo, today, represents a world-wide market of several billion dollars per year. He would have been even more gratified to know that epo was improving the lives of thousands of patients, most of whom will never hear the name Leon O. Jacobson or appreciate the value of his important contribution to their well-being.

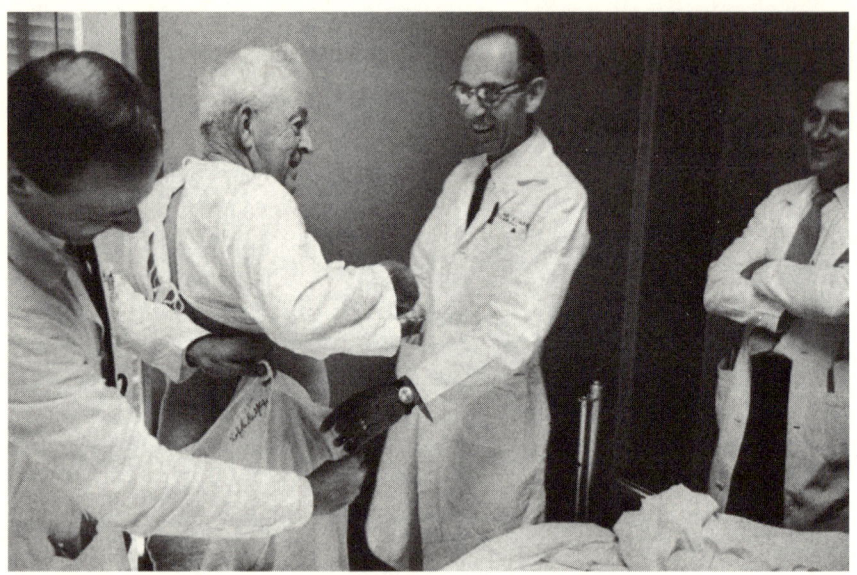

Jake with a patient and an unidentified colleague.

CHAPTER NINE

Administrator, Chairman, and Dean

". . . only one adminstrative head . . ."

As already indicated, Jake's ability as an administrator was recognized early, when he organized the clinical part of the Metallurgical Lab. The various university chairmen and deans were aware of the potential of the bright young doctor, and started to groom him for a career in academic medicine. In 1945, while still health officer of the Metallurgical Lab, he was appointed head of the Hematology section of the Department of Medicine, when the head at the time, Gurth Carpenter, left the university. The section was small and required very little effort on the part of its head, but it put Jake in fairly close contact with the university brass and made his appointment as Director of ACRH in 1951 almost automatic.

The combined roles as Director and section head suited his talents very well, and in both he was admired by his faculty colleagues for his lack of pretension and his always evident humor, as well as his occasional maverick behavior. He ran those units that he was responsible for with a style that was as far from the usual type of academic bureaucracy as could be imagined. He appointed people to the hematology faculty and ACRH without significant consultation with the staff of either group, but he did get the needed approval from the Dean's office or Department chair. He often relied on suggestions from friends and made the appointment before anyone was aware of what was happening. During this period, Jake's outside activities included being named twice to be the technical advisor to the U.S. delegation to the International Conference on Peaceful Uses of Atomic Energy.

At about that time, Cog retired and a new dean, H. Stanley Bennett, was appointed. The Department of Medicine was in turmoil. The chairman, Dr. Wright Adams, had been rather lax in building the faculty and there was a general feeling that the department was in a precipitous decline. Adams resigned the chair and the search committee urged the dean to appoint Jake, who had not been on the search committee, to the chair. A poll of the faculty showed 29 of 40 in favor of Jake's appointment as chairman. After some hesitation, Jake agreed to serve, on condition that Richard Landau be named secretary of the department. Landau would then carry the burden of the day-to-day departmental matters. With Landau's agreement, Jake became chairman in 1961.

The turmoil in the department did not abate, and in fact got worse when Jake convinced the faculty to approve the appointment of Rudi Schmid as a tenured professor. Schmid was a protégé of Cecil Watson, a hematologist and good friend of Jake's. Schmid quickly set about trying to remake the department in terms of both structure and clinical responsibilities. He was supported by some of the junior faculty and opposed by Jake and the senior faculty, splitting the department into two opposing camps that carried on incessant intramural warfare. In a note to the faculty, Jake wrote: "In the past year I have received enough advice, both verbatim and written, from within and without our institution to fill several large volumes. After living or rather attempting to live with all this advice, I have finally locked it all in a file for reference and have emerged with the philosophy that this department—or any department—can have only one administrative head."

As the situation in the department deteriorated, Jake thought it had become intolerable and in a hand-written note to Dean Bennett, he said:

> ... In any event I am ready to step down from the chair of medicine without a qualm at this time. In other words I expect you to consider this letter as my resignation as Chairman of Medicine ...
>
> I have not recovered from the final realization of what I think was stupidity on my part in accepting the chair of medicine. I guess I was deluded by the idea expressed by some of my colleagues that I was the only solution for the department. Now I can see more

clearly after these two years that someone with a fresh point of view, unimpaired by emotional ties could have done better.

His resignation was not accepted and eventually things cooled down. Schmid was disarmed and his faction gave up trying to remodel the department. Jake had relied on his friendship with the members of the department to support him, and was disappointed that they did not all do so.

In almost all of his dealings with colleagues, he wanted to be loved and to have his views accepted. When he thought he had failed, his solution was to retire from the fray and give up the job. His distaste for the wrangling took the form, on occasion, of his simply leaving a department meeting and relying on Richard Landau to take over. In December of 1964, Dean Bennett wrote to the Provost (Edward Levi), recommending that Jake be reappointed as chairman after his first three-year term was up. He said that faculty opinion was "bimodal," with senior faculty indicating that Jake pressed too rapidly and radically for change, while the junior faculty argued that he did not press fast enough. He was appointed to a second term but served only one year of it. The remainder of his chairmanship was characterized by his being somewhat aloof from departmental matters, essentially letting Landau administer the department. He did, however, keep aware of what was happening, as this memo he sent to the whole departmental faculty illustrates:

> This is the University of Chicago, and the medical school and hospitals exist in fact for the specific purpose of education and research: patients are not to be treated as things or animals but rather as human beings who have come to the University of Chicago hospital for university hospital type care . . . (they) are to receive the ultimate in medical care.

Over the years of devoting the bulk of his time and effort to administration and research, he never lost his passion for patient care. In a note to himself, he once wrote: I've enjoyed everything I've ever done but I've always been a doctor first. I loved my patients and I loved teaching." In his case, teaching and patient care were parts of the same effort. He taught at the bedside with medical students and residents at his side. Once, when with such a group around him, he asked one of them to lend him $20. One of the patients they had been examining was an elderly lady of little means and Jake wanted to give her some money so she could take a taxi home. He explained that she had once run a boarding house for medical students and was known to be good to them. Not only was he devoted to his patients, they were devoted to him. His files are replete with letters from patients and their relatives brimming over with gratitude to him and often accompanied by checks to support his research.

In 1964, the five-year term of Dean Bennett had one more year to run. In accordance with university policy a committee was selected to recommend to the president and provost whether he should be reappointed to another term. There was considerable dissatisfaction with the dean from both the clinical and the basic science faculty, and many of them made it known to the chairman of that committee, L.O. Jacobson, that they were opposed to a second term. Jake was ambivalent. He was in favor of replacing Bennett because he felt that Bennett was inept, "... in over his head ...," and neglected the basic science part of the division, "... yet doesn't quite grasp the problems in the clinical areas...." In spite of his perception of these failings, Jake let the administration know of his reluctance to search for a new dean because of the difficulties involved.

There was a (possibly apocryphal) bit of university folklore about Jake going to tell Provost Edward Levi that the committee wanted a new dean. Knowing how prickly Bennett could be, Levi is supposed to have told Jake that he was to tell Bennett of that decision. Jake then told Levi that that was not his job, but it was the job of the Provost.

The same committee then met, without Jake in the chair, and recommended to Levi that Jake be appointed dean. Some senior members of the department met privately with George Beadle, the President, to urge the same thing. In a letter written ten years later to Charles Dunlap at Tulane, Jake reminisced about that time.

> One day I got a call from George Beadle and soon thereafter I was in his office with Ed Levi at his side. George was in shirtsleeves and Levi was dressed immaculately as usual with his usual bowtie. George said, "Jake I want you to be the dean." I tried to tell him and Ed that number one I didn't want to be a dean and secondly I was having the greatest time of my life teaching, taking care of my patients and running a reasonably productive laboratory. George retorted that he

wouldn't accept a no. He went on to say. "Listen Jake, you son-of-a-bitch, you and others convinced me to leave Cal Tech where I was comfortably situated, to be President of this University. So how can you, as a member of this faculty refuse to work with me." I tried other approaches like "I've been running things for years but only in times of plenty and I'm not sure I'd be worth a damn when money becomes scarce etc." I even told him that I was inarticulate, cussed a lot, drank whiskey etc., but it was no go. I must say, however, that working with George and Ed Levi and eventually with Ed Levi and John Wilson was a stimulating experience.

It is interesting that in this recollection of that meeting ten years earlier, he seems to have forgotten how much trouble he had as department chairman at that time.

Jake accepted the appointment, resigned the chair, and prepared himself for the deanship while Bennett was still in office. Once he took on the duties as dean, he appointed several Associate Deans to distribute the administrative burdens, but kept decision-making in his own hands. Most of the Associate Deans had responsibilities but no budgetary authority, which made the position less attractive than the name would imply. In a few cases, Associate Deans were appointed without a clear idea of what their roles were to be. Jake once asked a friend on the faculty just what one particular Associate Dean did, and then asked that Dean what he was supposed to be doing. Jake seemed to view his office as the locus of fund-raising for the Division and spent lots of time wooing potential donors.

The Division of Biological Sciences had for many years contained the clinical departments with the attached hospitals and what were then termed the "Preclinical," now the Basic Science, departments. Previous deans had concentrated on the former, letting what had been a distinguished basic science faculty be hired away, or not replaced upon retirement. Jake was concerned about this decay in the basic sciences and appointed Richard Lewontin, an eminent evolutionary biologist, as Associate Dean for the Basic Sciences. Lewontin was told that the resources of the division, in part due to hospital income, were at the service of the whole division, and that he was to have autonomy and act, in essence, as a co-dean. Reversing the effects of years of neglect was neither easy nor very successful, although a few units did flourish.

When he left to take a position at Harvard, Lewontin was replaced by Robert Uretz, who had been Chairman of the Biophysics Department. Uretz was first appointed as Associate Dean, then as Deputy Dean. He had the authority to deal directly with the Provost on academic matters, including salaries, which at Chicago were negotiated with the person, the chairman, the dean, and the provost.

With the new structure in place, Jake devoted himself to trying to build up the basic biological sciences which, as noted, had been neglected by his predecessors in favor of a number of new hospitals built over a relatively short time. The sorry state of the physical facilities for the basic sciences convinced Jake that recruitment of high-quality biologists would not be possible with such poor laboratories, and that retaining faculty members who were quite eminent was very difficult when competing institutions could promise much better working conditions. He then set about finding funds and space for a new biology building on campus. This had been one of Bennett's plans and there was a promising start because of funding provided by the National Institutes of Health and the Ford Foundation. Bennett, however, had plans for a much more grandiose facility and did not act to use the funds in hand. The NIH had a change in policy that stopped all support for building projects and the Ford Foundation, seeing no action resulting from their grant, asked the university to return the funds. When he became dean, Jake was determined to go ahead with the new building regardless. It would house four basic science departments in an eleven-story structure on a site close to the hospitals, and was estimated to cost $9.5 million. The Ford money had been $2.5 million and the NIH $3.8 million, so that a total of $6.3 would now have to be found. This set-back did not deter Jake; he was determined to go ahead. He wrote to John Wilson, the then president of the university as follows: "Dear John   I just want to tell you that if the architects office persists in goofing up our Biological Science building plans or schedule I'm going to go back to the clinics and my lab. Love Jake." Jake then convinced Mr. Nathan Cummings to donate some of the needed funds and he used some of the $12 million donated to the medical school, in return for it being named the Pritzker School of Medicine, for the remainder.

Jake had gotten faculty approval for the selling of the name of the medical school but received an immense amount of flack from medical alumni for it. The new lab building, called the Cummings Life Science

Center, was opened in 1973, with two floors left unfinished because of lack of money.

With his move from the chair of medicine to the dean's office there was, inevitably, a vacancy in the chair of the department. The usual search committee was constituted and eventually came up with the names of three well-known and highly regarded medical scientists as candidates. In a most unusual practice, Jake visited each one at his own institution without bringing them to see and be seen by the faculty. He made some offers, but none of the three accepted the position. Jake then appointed Dr. Alvin Tarlov to the chair. Tarlov was a member of the medicine faculty but was not a very distinguished medical scholar. He was not the choice of either the senior or the junior members of the faculty. The faculty was surprised and puzzled by Jake's choice, because the chance was lost to import a high-level investigator or administrator. Speculation abounded as to Jake's motive; the supposition with the longest staying power was that Tarlov was chosen because he was compliant and that meant Jake could continue to run the department.

Jake, winter 1989/90, at ease in his retirement. Photo by Tunnell.

CHAPTER TEN

Jake the Person

"I've enjoyed everything I've ever done, but I've always been a doctor first. I loved my patients and I loved teaching."

Besides innovative scientific research on blood cell formation, distinguished academic administration at many levels, teaching that inspired many students, and devoted clinical care of patients, what else was there about Jake that merits comment? What was he like as a person, apart from the several roles he played in his career as doctor, scientist, administrator, and teacher?

Jake presented a public persona of "aw shucks, I'm just a kid off the ranch" and he made sure to cultivate that informal, laid-back, simple personality. He was, in fact, a complex person with characteristics such as insecurity, drive, organizing ability and perseverance shared by many successful scientist-administrators as well as businessmen who have to balance several roles in their lives. He was well aware of the singularity of his accomplishments, in some way parallel to those of George Beadle, who was president of the University of Chicago when Jake was Dean. Beadle was another boy off the farm, in his case, in Nebraska, who became a Nobel Laureate geneticist, and who built a world-class biology department at the California Institute of Technology before coming to Chicago. He also retained much of the aura of a farmer in the big city.

Betty and Jake at first lived on his income, which, even at that time during the Great Depression, must have been not far above the poverty line. She got a job in the Chicago Relief Administration as a nutritionist and her income became an important supplement to his as an intern: together they earned about $1,800 per year. In 1941, they decided that there was enough income for them to start a family, after moving to a two-bedroom apartment near the hospital. In their 1937 Chevrolet, they took a vacation, driving to North Dakota to the Sims ranch and then to South Dakota and Wyoming. While on this trip, Betty became car-sick and they realized that the first of their intended children was on the way. Eric was born on March 13, 1942. Their income increased with his position at the Metallurgical Lab and they lived comfortably if not lavishly. Somewhat later, they accumulated enough money to buy a house on Diamond Lake near Cassopolis in southern Michigan and it became the center of their summer vacations.

The then chief of hematology, Gurth Carpenter, told Jake that a future in academic medicine could only be undertaken by someone with a considerable independent income, and that he knew that Jake and Betty were not wealthy enough for such a life. Betty's father had been an academic economist before going into the government and she knew what that life entailed. In their discussions of their future, Jake came down strongly on the side of staying in academic medicine. They jointly arrived at an estimate of the income needed for a home, children and their education of $5,500 per year, and decided it could be done. Jake's salary increased slowly as academic salaries do but his promotions were more rapid than usual, so that they never questioned their decision to stay in academe. They became regular patrons of the Chicago Symphony Orchestra and Lyric Opera. They also belonged to the Chicago Council on Foreign Relations. Jake and Betty were at ease in their associations with the major tycoons of the Midwest and world-famous academics who were his colleagues

Jake did not take much time off from his many duties, but Betty and the kids spent a good part of the summer at their place on Diamond Lake. He went there on weekends and usually for a few weeks during the summer, and it provided him with a welcome escape from administrative headaches. He did a lot of maintenance work on the house and dock, and planted and picked a variety of berries for jam and jelly making. These included black and red raspberries, buffalo berries, choke cherries, June berries, strawberries, and blueberries. Sometimes the whole family pitched in with this activity, but most of the time it was Jake and Eric who produced a very large amount of jams and jellies, which they shared with friends and neighbors. Jake also gave preserves to volunteer organizations associated with the University hospital, which then sold them at bazaars. He indicated how surprised he was at the high prices they got for his berry jams.

In his other hobby, woodworking, he learned how to cure green wood chemically rather than having to use the more expensive method of kiln drying. He also learned about people from nearby wood-lots who bought trees for making planks and then either sold for firewood or gave away those parts of the tree not suitable for straight boards. He generally used woods such as black walnut, cherry, ash, maple mulberry, and osage orange (which he sometimes called iron wood), all of which were indigenous to that part of the Midwest. Depending on what he had in mind for the project, he might buy exotic woods such as teak, ebony, or rosewood. With the array of tools he had in the garage, he made tables, chairs, picture frames, or lamps. He also devoted considerable time to non-representational sculpture that he gave to friends. In retirement his wood-carving hobby occupied a lot of his time.

In January of 1967, there was an historic snowstorm in Chicago. The city was not prepared for the very heavy snow and was almost completely paralyzed. Jake lived within walking distance of the university hospital and made rounds of every nursing division and the blood bank several times a day over two twenty-four hour periods.

In his later years, when his career had crested and his scientific work was non-existent, he tended to look to the past rather than living in the present. An element of insecurity, which was part of his nature but most of the time was kept far beneath the surface, began to emerge. The humble beginning of his life showed through in the form of an almost compulsive trait of name-dropping, as though to remind his listeners about all the famous people he knew and to emphasize that his status was on the level of those people, despite his being a farm boy from North Dakota. Although it had increased as he aged it, was not a new development. As early as 1967, at age 56, in his voluminous letters to friends, donors, alumni, and relatives he almost always included an account of the trip he and Betty made to Stockholm on the occasion of the awarding of the Nobel prize in Physiology or Medicine to his friend and colleague Charles B. Huggins. It must have been important to Jake because he referred to it over and over again. The boy off the ranch seemed to still be trying to establish his bona fides by telling people of all the famous scientists, physicians, entertainers, politicians, and royalty he had encountered.

There were times, however, when he lost sight of reality. In a letter responding to a question about his career from a young high school student in North Dakota, he told her that he had "discovered" erythropoietin. Similarly, he wrote to someone that he and Robert Hutchins (the then president of the University) were friends and that he had taken the Great Books course offered by Hutchins and Mortimer Adler. His acquaintance with Hutchins was minimal, at best, during the war years at the Metallurgical Lab, and it strains credulity to believe that he could have found time to take that course when he was in medical school or as an intern, or when he was overwhelmed with his duties as health officer. With his North Dakota friends and relatives, he could not resist the temptation to make sure, in a low-key manner, that they realized his importance. In 1969, on the occasion of a reunion of the Almont High School students, he wrote in a letter to a friend, "As you know I am the Dean of the Medical School here at the University of Chicago and it is fearsome responsibility involving an annual budget of about $58 million."

In contrast to these indications of uncertainty about his accomplishments, reminiscences of former students and faculty members have a recurring theme emphasizing his comfort in his position. One frequent theme tells of Jake meeting someone—a student, faculty member or technician—draping his arm around that person's shoulder and inviting him (it almost always was a male) for coffee and a chat. On one occasion, he and I went to the hospital cafeteria to have some coffee and to talk about research. The place was full, and the only seats we could find were at a table already occupied by a nurse. Jake recognized her from his days as an intern and proceeded to tell her how important she had been in his medical education and reminded her of a few small details that were still in his memory so many years later. She was relatively silent, not commenting on what the dean was saying, finished her coffee, and left the table. Jake then realized that she had no idea of who he was. Nurses had no reason to recognize deans.

Long after they had left the university, former students would be surprised and pleased when Jake would recognize them and remember their names. Faculty members commented that Jake was the only dean they ever dealt with who would simply invite them to join him for a cup of coffee without any appointment or formality needed. His generosity toward students, technicians, and colleagues was not without some small degree of self-interest. He would frequently get books, papers, or grant proposals to review and would ask one of his associates to do the reviewing, but he still kept his name on as the reviewer.

His warmth with his patients was legendary. They loved him without reservation and he reciprocated. In a letter to a Mrs. Jodaitis, whose husband was his patient and who had died of Hodgkin's disease, he wrote, "As you know I get very much attached to my patients and sometimes it seems as though I were taking care of just a big family." In one of his many notes to himself, he wrote "I've enjoyed everything I've ever done but I have been a doctor first. I loved my patients and I loved teaching."

Jake never let an opportunity to raise funds pass him by. He once wrote to George Beadle about the wife of a patient visiting him in his office and seeing a copy of the journal *Modern Medicine* with his picture on the cover:

> One experience I had this afternoon should be passed on in the event the approach might be applicable to others on the faculty, including you. . . . I sold her an autographed copy of *Modern Medicine* . . . for $1000, extracted a pledge for an additional $9000 and sealed it with a kiss. She's really not good looking and is 70 years old.

His home life, on the surface, was without much turmoil. Despite her recurrent bouts of ill health due to diabetes, Betty provided a base of stability, especially for Eric and Judy, whose father was out of town very frequently. She died at age 68 in 1983. It is curious to note that, in his "autobiography," Jake wrote that ". . . Betty gave birth to a beautiful daughter Judith Ann." Both Jake and Judy spoke openly about the fact that Judy was adopted; her mother's name was Rita Fisher. Eric Jacobson claimed, to me, that Jake was indeed Judy's father.

Relations between Jake and the kids were at times stormy, especially with Eric, who had significant difficulties at school and college. By Eric's account, Jake was a strict taskmaster who had very high expectations and reacted badly when they were not met. This strictness extended even to the grandchildren.

If one accepts the concept that children recapitulate, as adults, some of their parents' behavior, John Jacobson must have set the pattern of a strict father. In his writings, Jake hardly ever mentions his father. Their home was a center of hospitality for the many academic and administrative colleagues visiting Jake, many of whom stayed with the

Jacobson family. For most of them, Betty hosted dinner parties in their home, with local colleagues invited as well.

After the children were old enough to be left on their own, Betty traveled with Jake, especially on trips to accept the many honors he received. Over the years, he delighted in telling the story of the time in 1976 when he and Betty went to Bismarck, where he was inducted by the governor of the state into the North Dakota Hall of Fame, and to receive the Teddy Roosevelt Rough Rider Award. On the way to Bismarck, they stopped in Fargo to visit friends from the time they were both students there. When they were leaving the plane in Fargo, they were surprised and pleased to see the university band on the tarmac playing. It was not an anticipated welcome and they expected the music to stop when they were on the ground. The band kept playing and Jake looked back only to see that the welcome was not for them but for a passenger getting off behind them, Lawrence Welk, the television champagne music man who was also an eminent North Dakotan. Jake said that Welk was smiling and waving to the assembled greeters while he and Betty melted into the crowd. Some years later, Jake wrote to Welk apologizing for using his name during the many tellings of the anecdote, because the person behind them was not Welk but a former bandmaster at North Dakota State University. In his letter, Jake explained that nobody would have recognized the name of the bandmaster, so he took the liberty of substituting Welk's first name. Welk wrote back to tell Jake that he wouldn't tell anyone if Jake also wouldn't.

Betty also went with him to Norway when he was made a Knight of the First Order by King Olaf and received the Gold Medal of Merit. These honors were especially important for Jake because of his attachment to Norway and the Norwegian language. He had devoted a good deal of time, effort, and money toward establishing a professorship in Norwegian studies at the university, as a tribute to his Norwegian forebears.

He had a large number of friends, but only a few were close. They were mostly University of Chicago faculty members and colleagues in Hematology at other institutions. He saw the latter fairly frequently at conferences and on his travels. They remember him as an engaging, humorous drinking companion, who socialized with them after the scientific work of the conference was done. At national and international meetings, Jake would be a generous host for dinners at upscale restaurants for his friends. He would be reimbursed from non-federal funds at his disposal, much to the annoyance of his secretary, who complained that he never kept receipts.

His friends also included some of the leading figures of Chicago industry and commerce, some of whom were also his patients and targets for his fund raising. Many of his patients remained in touch with him for years, long after they needed his clinical expertise. For example, Sid Luckman, a retired star football player for the Chicago Bears kept in contact and every year sent Jake season tickets for the Bears games. Jake generally gave the tickets to others.

His relationship with his coworkers was especially warm. Those who were close stayed with him for many years, reciprocating his affection for them. One illustration of how he dealt with his technicians came from Dr. Eric Simmons, who worked with Jake for more than 30 years. During the research on the "humoral hypothesis," the lab group set up a large experiment involving mice; for all of them it was a nonstop day in the lab. When Jake finished his morning clinical duties, he stopped by the lab to see how things were going and found them all hard at work, not having been able to break for lunch. They expected him to pitch in with the mouse work so they could stop soon and eat. Instead, he went to the brown bags containing the lunches and asked around, "Who has peanut butter? Who has tuna salad? etc." He then cut the sandwiches into bite-sized pieces and went around the room putting the pieces into each appropriate open mouth.

He made a practice of responding to essentially every letter he received, including notes of congratulations on his several promotions, and questions from people about medical problems, relatives of patients and people he never met but who knew of him through the media publicity and who wanted advice. He also wrote to politicians, alumni, and potential donors. Two examples demonstrate how he interacted with this latter group.

Mr. Ben May of Mobile, Alabama, was a wealthy benefactor of the University's Division of Biological Sciences, especially of Dr. Charles B. Huggins, for whom he established an endowed laboratory. Jake, the consummate practicing physician of vast clinical experience, had rather severe rheumatoid arthritis of both hands, which caused a lot of pain and limited use of his hands. Mr. May knew of the problem and advised Jake to take vitamin B-12 for it. Jake wrote, thanking him for the suggestion, and asked " What kind and size of dose do you think I should take?" It is very doubtful that he ever took any.

In an exchange of letters with Mr. Cyrus Eaton, the Cleveland industrialist and member of the university board of trustees, Jake discussed his disagreement with the ideas expressed by Jacques Monod in his book *Chance and Necessity*, saying that he could not accept Monod's view that there was no divine guidance. "Are there no values, no morality derivable independent of science? Can science help us perceive what we should seek to do; given our power of influencing evolution?" One may wonder whether this statement was tailored for Eaton, since during the many years I worked with him I never heard him mention divinity or religion and the phrase about evolution seems far out of context.

On occasion, he referred to evolution in a strange way. For example, in February of 1983, he wrote to W.T. Hoyt of the Council for Tobacco Research, which Jake chaired at that time, about a talk he had given the previous month and which he did not intend to publish. In that talk, he discussed what he saw as shortcomings of the Food and Drug Administration with regard to the delay in approving drugs for clinical use, a subject once again in the news. He also wrote that "... a little radiation may be good for us because it produces mutations, some of which are important in the evolutionary process." Most certainly he knew how far off base that statement was, having worked in radiation biology. He never would have said that to a scientific colleague.

Although in his adult life he was not a church-goer, the impact of religion in his early life left a strong residue of belief, even though it may have been unorthodox. At the 90th anniversary of the founding of the Sims Evangelical Lutheran Church, he wrote that his mother—who was, to her grandchildren, a very forceful woman—believed that only Christians could be "saved." He followed that statement with: "I cannot believe that God in his infinite wisdom and mercy ever determined at the time of Christ or since that non-Christians could achieve only the fate of the damned."

Eric Jacobson has told me that his father and his Jacobson uncles were all alcoholics. There is some evidence, in addition to Eric's own observations, that supports that statement, at least with respect to Jake.

In the University archives, among the collection of papers made available to me by Dr. Elise Torczinski, is a hand-written note to her, undated and unsigned but probably written in 1990. The writer was a patient of Dr. Torczinski's, who restored her sight, and who was very grateful to her. The note says:

> According to Rev. Seitz (St. Thomas the Apostle Church) with whom I discussed it (in the absence of Rev. Ferry) it is my duty and obligation to enlighten you, preferably before the pre-nuptial talks. Our mutual friend to who you are betrothed is alcoholic. While he is a brilliant scientist and a respected friend he "denies" his problem and adroitly hides it denying it particularly to himself.
>
> Family and friends are powerless to aid him although they are painfully aware of the destruction it is causing . . .

In another note in Jake's own collection of papers in the archive, Jake's brother Raymond wrote to him; "Never realized how well life goes on without cocktails and martinis."

Those of us who were with him, away from Chicago at conferences and meetings, could easily see how much he could and did drink without our detecting any effect. There was, however, one instance when I was with him at the Detroit airport waiting for him to return to Chicago while I stayed on for a few days. The plane was delayed and we sat in the lounge drinking. He got so drunk on martinis that he could hardly stagger to the plane when it was called. In spite of all this, to the best of my knowledge and of others who worked with him, he never was under the influence of alcohol while at work. After his retirement, he occasionally would wander into the office of a colleague with a clear indication that he had been drinking shortly before.

In his pursuit of potential donors, Jake was unstinting of time and effort. There is a curious set of handwritten, undated notes to him, probably written between 1965 and 1972, from a possible donor on whom he lavished a great deal of attention: Mrs. Adelaide Seeberger (later called Seeger). They are curious because they are one-sided, with no responses from him, and more pointedly because they suggest, from her point-of-view, a very personal relationship between them in his fund raising activity. Many of her notes open with the phrase "Please read and destroy" and are addressed to "cherie" and signed "me." For some reason, Jake kept them and included them in his collected papers, which are stored in the university archives. She clearly expected Jake to help her in her loneliness and complained frequently about his lack of attention to her after a period when they appeared to be quite close. Jake lent his car and driver to take her shopping and to the airport when she traveled and she used his secretary to pick up prescriptions for her as well as to get stamps. She was well aware that Jake wanted a substantial donation from her and she used it as a bargaining chip to get him to pay more attention to her. In one of her notes, she complained of hurt feelings:

> . . . while it started with the wedding where there were more lies on lies and ended with asking me for Sear's stock. By this time you should know you can't fool Adelaide and that I have a mind of my own. This was inexcusable (and I am thinking of buying a 100 000 non-refundable annuity).

On occasion she would refer with some poignancy to the "happy days of fund raising" and to some incident on the "toll road" that had much meaning for her but was never explicated. Her moods in these notes ranged from kittenish to doting to querulous to fed up. At one point Jake, wrote to someone in the development office that he thought he had ". . . lost Adelaide." In her will, she left at least $800,000 to the university.

His addiction to nicotine was well known. At one time, when Stanley Bennett was Dean and ruled that there was to be no smoking at Divisional meetings, Jake would ostentatiously stand at the back of the room and light up a cigarette. He stopped smoking many times and took up a pipe, only to give it up in short order and return to cigarettes. When questioned about why he smoked, given the preponderance of evidence of the potential harm, his response almost invariably was "It's only statistics."

He served on the Tobacco Research Council from 1954 to 1991 and chaired its scientific advisory board for many years. This organization was looked on by some as a way for the industry to counter the bad publicity around the question of lung cancer and heart attacks due to smoking. Jake, perhaps, thought it might make his addiction less threatening but devoted much time and effort to the committee. In one note that he wrote, he asked ". . . why such great emphasis was given to smoking rather than to other environmental insults?" At one time when he indicated his wish to retire from the board, Luther Terry, the Surgeon General of the United States, asked him to stay on the

Tobacco Research Council so that someone on the council would have "no axe to grind." On his retirement from the Tobacco Research Board, one person said that ". . . they distributed $18 million in basic science support through the year 1991 and have high hopes for higher (increased) budget for the next year. We are now among the top ten granting agencies supporting biomedical research in the country. A large part of the credit belongs to you." In a letter written by Charles Sommers in 1992, the writer stated that "He ran the meetings firmly, with aplomb and good humor . . . The group of disparate disciplines and in some cases big egoes(sic) recognized and respected his leadership. Jake endured the criticism and in the early years the obloquy that went with the job, with his usual customary good rational composure." What a change from his chairing of department meetings!

Jake at 80.

CHAPTER ELEVEN

Last Days

*"Now I'll just be around and one of you.
I'm happy in my new freedom."*

After retiring as Dean and Director of ACRH, Jake continued to see patients but to a much reduced extent. In September of 1982, he wrote to the then chairman and the secretary of the Department of Medicine to tell them he had decided to stop seeing patients because liability insurance, which amounted to $2,000 per year, was more than he wanted to spend, and ". . . over the years as Dean etc. I have found it difficult to keep up with the rapid and great changes in medicine. Consequently I am a little uncomfortable about continuing to take responsibility for patients. Actually I haven't been seeing many patients and have referred the complicated ones to Resnekov, Gurney and others." He continued to keep an office in the hospital where he wrote the talks he would deliver at various ceremonial events, but would not publish.

As he devoted less time to clinical duties, the time available for his wood-carving hobby increased. Over the years, his arthritic condition worsened and his hands were kept in braces to reduce painful movement. The drugs he was taking also had unpleasant side-effects and he generally suffered them all stoically.

His loneliness, since Betty's death, was exaggerated when he no longer had administrative and clinical duties to keep himself occupied. His role in experimental science had ended some years earlier and he had not made much effort to keep up with the latest findings in the fields he had done so much to advance. Eric and Judy and their children were not living in Chicago and he had time with them only on holidays or during the summer at the house in Michigan.

In 1990, after about two years of "dating," he married a second time, to Dr. Elise Torczinski, who was his ophthalmologist. His children and friends commented on how happy Elise had made him. They were married in a Catholic ceremony at St. Thomas the Apostle Church in the University neighborhood. Elise is a practicing Catholic and Jake had no objection to being one, even though he was not a Catholic himself.

In 1992, a year after his 80th birthday, in conjunction with the 100th anniversary of the founding of the University there was a belated scientific symposium and dinner in his honor on the University campus. The symposium speakers were all former students, research collaborators, or faculty members who had served under his leadership in ACRH, on the hematology service, or in the Department of Medicine. He sat in the front row of the lecture hall with Elise, both hands done up in braces, but never asked any questions or made any comments. It was clear that he was moved by the tributes to him but seemed to be rather dissociated. Perhaps it was due to his learning that Eric had been diagnosed with a meningeal tumor and needed brain surgery. Eventually, Eric made a complete recovery. Another part of his lack of affect may have been due to the general decline in cognitive function he was experiencing.

Jake and Elise agreed to live in her apartment, leaving the one she described as ". . . rather barren, just a bit of furniture. A few nice pictures, some knik-nacks. Needs a woman's touch." Several months after they were married, they agreed to a financial "arrangement" with the following terms: Elise would pay 90% of the rent, the other 10% Jake would pay for his office. Costs of utilities, groceries, newspapers, telephone, cable TV service, cleaning and laundry would be split 50:50. Jake would pay for entertainment and dining out. Other expenses such as upkeep of the car would be negotiated.

For a while there was some friction between Elise and Jake on the one hand and Eric and Rita on the other about the Michigan house. It was resolved with the understanding that there would be "private" space for each couple and shared space for both. After it was worked out Jake, sent a note to Rita saying, "Forgive me if I was harsh and abrupt with you."

Jake started to work seriously on his will, but complained that he could not understand wills. He used the backs of envelopes to compose tentative wills, with significant uncertainty about how to divide his assets between Judy and Eric. Some of the issues were resolved when he decided that Eric should inherit the Michigan house and that Judy and her husband would be compensated by having the sizable loan Jake had made to them, to permit them to buy a house, forgiven.

Jake's physical and mental condition steadily worsened, with obvious symptoms of debilitation. His memory became vague, he was easily disoriented, and even got lost in the corridors of the hospital that he had walked for some 60 years.

He died unexpectedly and peacefully at home at 5:00 P.M. on September 20, 1992, after taking a deep breath. Elise, Eric, and Judy were with him. Death was caused by coronary artery disease with accompanying carcinoma of the lung with metastases in the brain, along with several fairly serious other lesions.

Elise arranged a "Viking" funeral for Jake in which the casket and grave received "gifts" for the afterlife; these included a model Viking ship that he got when he was knighted in Norway, a candlestick made by his brother Melvin, a tomato to commemorate his Michigan garden, a jar of Michigan berry jelly, a tape of his favorite songs, a vial of nitrogen mustard, a "mouse," some earth and water from Diamond Lake, a magazine, a cigarette lighter, a limerick, a coffee cup, a soft pillow, pencil and paper, and some seeds from his garden. In addition, a cigarette was placed in his jacket pocket and a pack in the coffin.

As was mentioned, those who knew Jake will remember him first for his imagination and sense of humor, his friendship and informality, his extraordinary openness, even as dean, to students and colleagues, and his limitless compassion for his patients.

Index of Names

Adams, Dr. Wright, 58
Adler, Mortimer, 68
Alexander, Dr. S. F., 3
Almont High School, 10, 13, 68
Archer, Shreve, 22, 23
Argonne Cancer Research Hospital (ACRH), 1, 40, 41–45, 48, 50, 57, 77, 78
Argonne National Lab, 38, 40, 41, 44
Armour and Company, 53–54
Atomic Energy Commission (AEC), 38, 39

Bachmeyer, Dr. Arthur C., 25
Bari, Italy, 2, 3
Beadle, George, 60, 61, 65, 69
Bennett, H. Stanley, 58, 59, 60, 61, 74
Benton, Alva, 18, 22
Bethard, Dr. William, 49
Bloom, Prof. William, 23, 24
Bly, Col. E. H., 7, 8
Bush, Vannevar, 38

Cancer Isotope Hospital, 39
Cannon, Dr. 24
Carnot, Paul, 47
Carpenter, Gurth, 57, 66

Coggeshall, Dr. Lowell T. (Cog), 37, 38, 39, 40, 58
Cold War, 32, 50
Cole, Dr. Kenneth C., 27
Compton, Arthur H., 25, 38
Cummings, Nathan, 62
Cummings Life Science Center, 62–63
Cunningham, Sir Arthur, 2

Darwin, Charles, 34
Deflandre, Camille, 47
Denoyer, Charles, 10, 14
Department of Energy, 44
Diamond Lake, Michigan, 66, 79
Dick, Dr. George B., 4, 23, 24, 25
Dirksen, Sen. Everett, 40
Dragstedt, Lester, 23
Dunlap, Charles, 60

Eaton, Cyrus, 72
ERDA, 44
Erythropoietin (epo), 47–50, 53–55

Fargo, North Dakota, 15, 18
Fermi, Enrico, 26, 27, 38
Fisher, Rita, 69
Food and Drug Administration, 72
Ford Foundation, 62

Index of Names

Franklin McLean Research Institute, 44
Frederika, Queen of Greece, 45
Fried, Walter, 48, 49

Gaston, Evelyn, 27, 41, 48, 53
Gilman, Dr. Alfred S., 5
Gold Medal of Merit (Norway), 70
Goldwasser, Eugene, 43
Gottschalk, Dr. Alexander, 44
Groves, General Leslie, 37
Gurney, Clifford, 50, 77

Hannafin, Dennis, 7
Harrison, R. Wendall, 37
Harvey, Dr. Basil, 24
Harwell, 33, 34
Hilberry, Norman, 25, 26
Hodges, Dr. Clarence, 23, 25, 26
Hoyt, W. T., 72
Huggins, Charles B., 24, 67, 71
Humphreys, Dr., 24
Hutchins, Robert M., 38, 68

Institute of Nuclear Studies, 38
International Conference on Peaceful Uses of Atomic Energy, 58

Jacobson, Arnold, 9
Jacobson, Mrs. Charley, 15
Jacobson, Clarence, 9
Jacobson, Elizabeth Benton (Betty), 18–19, 24, 65, 66, 67, 69, 70, 77
Jacobson, Eric, 66, 69, 77, 78, 79
Jacobson, John, 8, 9, 69
Jacobson, Judith Ann (Judy), 69, 77, 79
Jacobson, Maurice, 9
Jacobson, Melvin, 9, 79
Jacobson, Rachel Johnson, 8, 9, 15
Jacobson, Raymond, 9, 73
Jacobson, Rita, 78
Jacobson, Robert, 9
Jacobson, Thalia, 9
Jenner, Edward, 36
Jodaitis, Mrs., 69
John Harvey (American Liberty ship), 2–3
Johnson, Arion, 8

Kirsner, Joseph, 23
Knight of the First Order (Norway), 70
Kuratowskà, Zofia, 50
Kuratowski, Kasimir, 50

Ladd, Dr. Culver, 16, 21
Landau, Richard, 58, 59
Leopold Schepp Foundation, 22
Levi, Edward, 59, 60, 61
Lewontin, Richard, 61, 62
Lilienthal, David, 40
Lorenz, Egon, 34
Loutit, John, 34
Luckman, Sid, 71
Lushbaugh, Dr. Clarence, 3, 4

Manhattan Project, 26, 27, 28, 37
Marks, Edna K., 27, 28, 41, 48, 53
Masserman, Dr. Jules, 23
May, Ben, 71
McLean, Dr. Franklin, 4, 23, 44
McMahon, Sen. Brian, 39
Metallurgical Lab, 1, 23, 26, 27, 30, 37, 38, 48, 57, 66
Monod, Jacques, 72
Murray, Dr. Joseph E., 29

Nakao, Dr. Kiku, 49
National Cancer Institute (NCI), 39
National Institutes of Health (NIH), 39, 53–54, 62

Index of Names

North Dakota Agricultural College, 15, 18, 21
North Dakota Hall of Fame, 70
North Dakota State Regulatory Department, 16
North Dakota Superintendent of Public Instruction, 16

Oak Ridge National Lab, 40
Office of Naval Research, 38

Palmer, Walter, 23
Pasteur, Louis, 36
Plzak, Louis, 48, 49
Porsche, Dr., 34
Pritzker School of Medicine, 62

Rabi, Isidore, 38
Reserve Officers Training Corps, 16
Resnekov, Dr., 77
Rothman, Stephen, 23
Rowley, Dr. Janet, 42–43
Rush Medical College, 23

Salk, Jonas, 36
Scandinavian Evangelical Lutheran Church (Sims, ND), 7, 10, 72
Scheele, Leonard, 39
Schmid, Rudi, 58, 59
Seeberger, Adelaide, 73–74
Simmons, Dr. Eric, 27, 28, 42, 71
Sims, North Dakota, 7
Sims, George, V., 8
Sims, William S., 8
Smith, Dr. Taylor, 4
Sommers, Charles, 75
Spurr, Dr. Charles, 4

Steiner, Dr., 24
Stone, Dr. Robert, 27
Straus, L., 40
Swarm, John, 7
Szilard, Leo, 27, 32–33

Taliaferro, William H., 25, 37
Tarlov, Dr. Alvin, 63
Teddy Roosevelt Rough Rider Award, 70
Terry, Luther, 74
Thomas, Dr. E. Donnall, 29, 35, 36
Thompson, C. J., 8
Tobacco Research Council, 72, 74–75
Torczinski, Dr. Elise, 72–73, 78, 79
Toxicity Laboratory, 1–2, 4, 44

University of Chicago Cancer Research Foundation, 38
University of Chicago Hospital, 1
University of Chicago School of Medicine, 19, 21
Uretz, Robert, 62

Vandenburg, Sen. Arthur, 39

Watson, Cecil, 58
Welk, Lawrence, 70
Wells, Dr., 24
Willman, Andrew, 10
Wison, John, 61, 62
Wintrobe, Maxwell, 5
Woolan, Ernest, 25, 26

Zirkle, Ray, 28
Zubrod, C. G., 3